NANCY HARRIS

Nancy Harris is an award-winning playwright from Dublin. Theatre credits include *The Beacon* (Druid/Gate Theatre Dublin); *The Red Shoes* (Gate Theatre, Dublin); *Our New Girl* (Bush Theatre, London/Atlantic Theater, New York); *No Romance* (Peacock Theatre, Dublin); *Love In A Glass Jar* (Peacock Theatre, Dublin); *Baddies: The Musical* (Unicorn Theatre, London); *Journey to X* (National Theatre Connections); *The Kreutzer Sonata* (Gate Theatre, London/La Mama, New York).

Nancy received the Rooney Prize for Irish Literature and the Stewart Parker Award for her debut full-length play *No Romance* in 2012. She was a finalist for the Susan Smith Blackburn Award. She has also written for radio and television and was nominated for a BAFTA as a Breakthrough Talent in 2014 for her writing on the Channel 4 series *Dates*.

Nancy Harris

TWO LADIES

NICK HERN BOOKS

London

www.nickhernbooks.co.uk

A Nick Hern Book

Two Ladies first published in Great Britain in 2019 as a paperback original by Nick Hern Books Limited, The Glasshouse, 49a Goldhawk Road, London W12 8QP

Two Ladies copyright © 2019 Nancy Harris

Nancy Harris has asserted her right to be identified as the author of this work

Cover image: Zoë Wanamaker and Zrinka Cvitešić; art direction: Muse Creative Communications; photographer: Perou

Designed and typeset by Nick Hern Books, London
Printed in the UK by Mimeo Ltd, Huntingdon, Cambridgeshire PE29 6XX

A CIP catalogue record for this book is available from the British Library

ISBN 978 1 84842 881 2

Woodland
CARBON
www.woodlandcarbon.co.uk
NICK HERN BOOKS
Printed on Carbon Captured paper

Two Ladies was first performed at the Bridge Theatre, London, on 25 September 2019. The cast was as follows:

HELEN	Zoë Wanamaker
SOPHIA	Zrinka Cvitešić
GEORGES	Yoli Fuller
SANDY	Lorna Brown
FATIMA	Raghad Chaar
UNDERSTUDY *to Helen*	Julia Righton
UNDERSTUDY *to Georges*	Dimitri Jeannest
UNDERSTUDY *to Sophia, Sandy and Fatima*	Ann Marcuson

Director	Nicholas Hytner
Designer	Anna Fleischle
Lighting Designer	Johanna Town
Sound Designer	George Dennis
Composer	Grant Olding
Assistant Director	Sean Linnen
Design Associate	Liam Bunster
Casting Director	Robert Sterne
Costume Supervisor	Ilona Karas
Wigs	Campbell Young
Props Supervisor	Lizzie Frankl
Production Manager	Marty Moore

Acknowledgements

My deepest thanks and appreciation to Nick Hytner for his
belief in and unwavering commitment to this play since its
very inception.

I am greatly indebted to he, and to Will Mortimer for their
insights, conversation and feedback throughout the writing
process.

I would also like to thank the following who were hugely
helpful to the research and development of this play at its
various stages:

Charlotte Wilkins for the French translation, Dan Muirden,
Nick McDonnell, Dave Evans, Anthony Weigh, Natalie
Radmall-Quirke, Julia Molony, Justine Mitchell, Sid Sagar,
Leaphia Darko, Wayne Jordan, Rochelle Stephens. I would also
like to thank Nick Starr and everyone at the Bridge Theatre.
And lastly, I would like to thank my beloved, Kwasi Agyei-
Owusu, for everything.

N.H.

For my mother, Anne, with love and gratitude

Characters

HELEN, *sixties – wife of the French President, English*
   (*pronounced Hélène at all times throughout the play*)
SOPHIA, *forties – First Lady of the United States, Croatian*
SANDY, *forties – press officer to the First Lady, American*
GEORGES, *thirties – press officer to the French President,*
   French
FATIMA, *twenties – a migrant to France, working as a catering*
   assistant, Syrian

Note on Text

A forward slash (/) indicates an overlap in dialogue.

Setting

A room on the first floor of a vast convention centre somewhere
on the Côte d'Azur.

Maybe a painting on the wall, but in essence we could be
anywhere.

A window.

Two chairs.

Some tables with some drinks.

The sense of a strong security presence outside the door.

A clock ticks constantly in the background – imperceptible at the
start, but growing louder as we go on. There is no clock onstage.

Outside this room, somewhere in the centre, an important
diplomatic meeting is taking place.

Time – any from now.

This text went to press before the end of rehearsals and so may
differ slightly from the play as performed.

Lights up on HELEN, *elegant, striking, exquisitely dressed,*
standing in the middle of the room.

Tense.

She has a drink in one hand.

Beat.

She downs it in one.

Then she goes to the window and looks out.

As the door bursts open, voices loud, a commotion –

SANDY (*into phone, fast, urgent*). No now. We need it *now.*
Tell them it's an emergency /

SOPHIA, *effortlessly glamorous, is led into the room*
wearing a pastel Chanel dress-suit. It is dramatically
covered with blood.

GEORGES (*to* SOPHIA, *guiding her*). This way, madame /

SANDY (*over him*). Cos it's *everywhere.* Literally. It literally
looks like someone blew his brains out on her suit – I said
the Chanel was a bad idea /

As GEORGES *offers* SOPHIA *a chair –*

GEORGES (*to* SOPHIA, *concerned*). Would you like to sit
down? /

SOPHIA *shakes her head, delicately.* SANDY *continues –*

SANDY. Well call Givenchy, call Stella, I don't – will she what?

SANDY *covers the phone, looks at* SOPHIA –

Will you wear vegan leather?

SOPHIA *looks like she doesn't understand.*

(*Into phone.*) She'll wear it if it gets here in ten – five! Oh
they are *not* boycotting, they just say that shit to look like
they've a conscience – and it's the conference centre right,

not the hotel, we got rerouted. Half the team's stuck across town. Yeah, real shit show.

She glances at GEORGES *and* SOPHIA.

Gotta go.

She hangs up.

No one seems to have noticed HELEN *for the moment.*

GEORGES. What did they say?

SANDY. They're sending something.

GEORGES. I mean about the –

He points to the blood on SOPHIA*'s dress.*

SANDY. Animal blood.

GEORGES (*shocked*). No!

SANDY. They'll run some more tests but she's not itching or coughing. (*To* SOPHIA.) No difficulty breathing?

SOPHIA *shakes her head.*

GEORGES. Who would do such a thing?

SANDY. Ask your President.

The sound of glass shattering behind.

They turn.

GEORGES. Hélène!

HELEN. Sorry. Lost my grip. /

SANDY. How did you get up here?

HELEN. I – walked.

SANDY. Walked! Like –

HELEN. On two legs, yes.

GEORGES (*rushing over*). But you are okay? The blood –

HELEN. Yes, yes I'm fine. Didn't get near me, I was lucky.

She looks at SOPHIA, *genuine.*

Are *you* alright?

SOPHIA *nods*.

What a terrible thing.

SANDY*'s on her phone*.

SANDY. Okay someone's put it up but it's grainy.

GEORGES *rushes over to look*. SOPHIA *seems anxious*.

GEORGES. A photograph?

SANDY. Film.

GEORGES. But the press were not permitted at the restaurant.

SANDY. But the protesters all have phones. Some don't have asylum in most of Europe but they got phones. (*To* HELEN, *dry*.) Bet your husband's glad he took a million.

A young CATERING ASSISTANT *comes to the door, looks inside tentative*.

CATERING ASSISTANT. Est-ce que quelqu'un veut du café?

SANDY. How did *she* get up here?

SANDY*'s about to have words with security*.

GEORGES. We requested some towels. (*To the* CATERING ASSISTANT.) Nous avons demandé des serviettes de toilette.

The CATERING ASSISTANT *looks confused*.

CATERING ASSISTANT.…. Serviettes? Mais je m'occupe de la restauration /

GEORGES (*urgent*). Rapidement, s'il vous plaît.

The CATERING ASSISTANT *rushes off*.

(*To* SANDY, *explaining*.) She is in catering so –

SANDY. We have a serious security situation, we can't just have people –

GEORGES. We bring the catering staff from Paris. They are all very highly screened.

SANDY *looks unconvinced*.

SANDY. Are there showers in this place?

GEORGES. Fourth floor.

SANDY. That's something.

She keeps texting as she goes to the window –

And they're gonna clear that street over there, right?

HELEN (*alarmed*). Why?

SANDY. Seriously?

HELEN. Well they've been arrested, haven't they? And you've got snipers on every roof across town. I mean –

SANDY. No one's gonna get shot today, okay. That would not be a good look right now.

HELEN *darts an irritated glance at* GEORGES, *before turning to* SOPHIA.

HELEN. Why don't you sit down?

SOPHIA. I am fine.

The CATERING ASSISTANT *comes back with a small towel.*

She holds it out, tentative.

CATERING ASSISTANT. J'ai trouvé… ça.

HELEN *points to* SOPHIA.

HELEN. Pour elle, s'il vous plaît.

GEORGES *snatches the towel off the* CATERING ASSISTANT.

GEORGES. Donnez-les moi.

He grandly presents it to SOPHIA, *all smiles.*

For you, madame.

SOPHIA *takes the towel coolly, starts to carefully wipe her dress.*

SOPHIA. Thank you.

GEORGES *points to the shattered glass on the floor.*

GEORGES (*to the* CATERING ASSISTANT, *curt*). Et nettoyez tout ça.

CATERING ASSISTANT (*nervous*). Je dois aller chercher la pelle.

GEORGES *eyes-rolls, impatient.*

GEORGES. Vite alors! /

The CATERING ASSISTANT *rushes out.* SANDY*'s on the phone.*

SANDY. Rudy, hi, what are we doing about these protesters?

GEORGES (*trying to get her attention*). I will speak to our security /

SANDY (*into phone*). Only another couple hundred. But we gotta get to a dinner later and it's basically a scene from *Carrie* here, only no one's going to the prom.

HELEN (*to* GEORGES, *irritated*). They're allowed to protest.

Something buzzes in SANDY*'s pocket.*

Another phone. She takes it out.

SANDY (*into phone*). Oh shit, it's headlining –

SOPHIA *looks up, alarmed.*

(*Into phone.*) I gotta come down there. (*To* SOPHIA, *curt.*) You okay for a minute?

SOPHIA. I –

SANDY. Great.

SANDY *heads out. As she leaves –*

We'll send the dress as soon as it gets here. (*To* SOPHIA.) Maybe try to look over that speech yeah, might relax you – (*To* GEORGES.) and no else is allowed up here, okay, great see you in a sec.

And she's gone.

HELEN *looks at* SOPHIA.

HELEN.…She's soothing.

She notices GEORGES *heading for the door.*

(*To* GEORGES, *slightly panicked.*) Where are *you* going?

GEORGES. There will be a briefing. I should probably –

HELEN. So you're just leaving – us?

HELEN *mouths 'me' then points to* SOPHIA *and mouths 'With her.'*

GEORGES *glances at* SOPHIA, *who is still wiping her legs.*

GEORGES. I will only be a few moments.

SOPHIA *glances up, quizzically.*

HELEN *quickly covers.*

HELEN. Course, yes. Actually, you know I might just try to grab a quick word with my husband –

GEORGES *stops.*

GEORGES. Your husband?

HELEN. About the press release. We had to travel in separate cars cos of all the commotion, we didn't have time to –

As she heads for the door –

GEORGES. But… the meeting has already started.

HELEN *stops, taken aback.*

HELEN. Started?

GEORGES. Ten minutes ago.

HELEN. But I thought – downstairs they said –

GEORGES. The First Lady did not want to delay things.

HELEN *glances at* SOPHIA.

HELEN. Oh.

GEORGES. And the Presidents were satisfied there's no further danger so…

GEORGES *smiles at* SOPHIA *who nods, gracious.*

Very generous.

HELEN *is visibly displeased.*

HELEN. Very. Generous.

She looks back at GEORGES.

So what, we're just –

GEORGES. Carrying on with the schedule, yes. Well as best we can – I will be back.

He goes.

HELEN *stares after him.*

HELEN. Carrying on with the schedule? Are they serious?

SOPHIA. It is better this way. I don't want to cause fuss.

She puts the towel down.

This is no good.

She straightens up, looks at HELEN, *who's still processing.*

HELEN. Well.

She takes in SOPHIA*'s blood-soaked clothes.*

…if anyone can carry it off, you can.

SOPHIA. Sorry?

HELEN. I was – joking. It was my very clumsy way of saying that you're handling all this excellently. With great – panache.

HELEN *smiles.*

Again, SOPHIA *doesn't.*

HELEN *looks around, a bit desperate. Spots the drinks on the table.*

(*Brightly.*) Would you like a drink? Someone's left a bottle of –

SOPHIA. No, thank you.

HELEN. Oh go on. Think you deserve it.

SOPHIA. Not when I am at work.

HELEN *stops.*

HELEN. Work? Ah yes. Easy to forget when you're not on the payroll.

SOPHIA *glances anxiously towards the door.*

SOPHIA. She did not show me the film.

HELEN. The – (*Realising.*) oh.

SOPHIA. I think it must be bad.

HELEN. I wouldn't worry too much. Think the papers have bigger things to chew on today, don't you?

SOPHIA. It is not the papers I am worried about. It is the Facebook. And the YouTube. And they can make a meme.

HELEN. Right.

SOPHIA. You have seen these?

HELEN. ...One or two.

SOPHIA. I hate these.

HELEN*'s not quite sure what to say.*

HELEN. Probably best not to think about it.

HELEN *moves to the window, looks out at the protesters in the distance.*

Suppose they've only themselves to blame really.

SOPHIA. Who?

HELEN. The newspapers. I mean look over there. Placards, children, dogs – one very lovely Dalmatian actually – but not one single reporter.

SOPHIA. How do you know?

HELEN. Cos they're all downstairs in the press area, aren't they? Waiting for official updates. Like veal calves waiting to be fed.

SOPHIA. You think they should be on the streets?

HELEN. Course they should be on the streets. They should be talking to those people, asking them questions – Who are you? Why have you come here? That's how you get a story. Not – scrolling through tweets...

SOPHIA. But we know why those people have come here.

    HELEN *turns*.

    It is all over my dress.

    And HELEN *suddenly remembers herself.*

HELEN. You know, I really think I should lend you something.

SOPHIA. No no –

HELEN. Our place isn't far, I'm sure they could –

SOPHIA. It is on its way.

HELEN. But honestly –

SOPHIA. And we are not the same size.

    HELEN *stops*.

HELEN....No.

    SOPHIA *gestures to the window.*

SOPHIA. I think you must miss this being a journalist, yes?

HELEN (*taken aback*). Me?

SOPHIA. The way you are talking. With such passion.

HELEN. Oh god, no. Just habit, that's all. Like a reflex. A gag one.

SOPHIA. Perhaps you will go back?

HELEN. To journalism? *When?*

SOPHIA. Someday.

HELEN. If there is one.

    An uncomfortable beat.

    HELEN *looks back towards the window.*

    Oh god, now it's snowing.

SOPHIA (*surprised*). On the Côte d'Azur?

HELEN. Hope you didn't bring your swimsuit. Or do you always have one? Just in case.

    SOPHIA *doesn't respond.*

I lost a stone, actually, when he got the job first. Had to, cos the women here are all like this –

She holds up a finger.

Like you in fact. And given I'm an interloper with the audacity of being from another country entirely, last thing I want is them talking about my big fat arse.

SOPHIA. They will always find something to talk about.

HELEN. True… Do you get used to it?

SOPHIA. Being an interloper?

HELEN. Being hungry all the time.

SOPHIA. I am not hungry.

HELEN. Well I am, I'm fucking starving.

SOPHIA. We have just had lunch.

HELEN. Well yes –

SOPHIA. But you did not eat much.

HELEN *looks up, surprised. Was she watching her?*

HELEN. No. Well I was doing so much talking, you know, to the new Chancellor.

SOPHIA. I find these summits – summits do you call it?

HELEN. It's what *they're* calling it, yes.

SOPHIA. I find it hard.

HELEN. Try being the wife of the host.

SOPHIA. Especially when things are so tense and everything is moving so quickly –

HELEN. Yes.

SOPHIA. And you have to make small talk in ten different languages with all these / men –

HELEN. Men, yes I know.

SOPHIA. And of course you are not the one they want to speak with. They want to speak with your husband.

HELEN. Well I'm sure some of them *much* prefer speaking to you.

SOPHIA *looks up, surprised.*

A quiet knock on the door. The CATERING ASSISTANT *hovers –*

CATERING ASSISTANT. Excusez-moi?

She holds up the dustpan.

CATERING ASSISTANT (*tentative*). Puis-je…

HELEN (*relieved*). Oui, oui bien sûr, entrez.

The CATERING ASSISTANT *stops briefly, eyes dropping to the blood on* SOPHIA*'s dress.*

Then she walks quickly over the broken glass.

The two ladies watch her, in lieu of making conversation.

The CATERING ASSISTANT *clearly feels self-conscious as she sweeps.*

HELEN *looks at her watch.*

How long do you think they'll be?

SOPHIA. They said a few minutes.

HELEN. They're quite capable of forgetting us you know.

SOPHIA. Really?

HELEN. Or losing us. Place is like a labyrinth – and every room looks the same. (*To the* CATERING ASSISTANT.) Did you happen to see any of our people – out there in that corridor?

The CATERING ASSISTANT *looks up.*

CATERING ASSISTANT. Hmmn?

HELEN (*repeating in French*).Y a-t-il quelqu'un dans le vestibule?

CATERING ASSISTANT. Vous voulez dire la securité?

HELEN (*to* SOPHIA). She thinks I mean security. / Non pas la –

The CATERING ASSISTANT *nods, effusively.*

CATERING ASSISTANT. Oui, il y a beaucoup de sécurité.

HELEN. Oh god, I've confused her now /

CATERING ASSISTANT. À chaque étage. *(To* SOPHIA, *kindly.)* Vous n'avez rien à craindre. Vous êtes à l'abri ici.

HELEN *smiles.*

HELEN. Well, that's sweet. *(To* SOPHIA.) She says you've nothing to worry about. You're quite safe here.

The CATERING ASSISTANT *nods at* SOPHIA, *smiles.*

SOPHIA *regards her, slightly suspiciously.*

HELEN *tries to make up for it.*

(To the CATERING ASSISTANT, *kind.)* Merci.

The CATERING ASSISTANT *does a little curtsy and goes out, glancing at* SOPHIA *as she goes.*

HELEN. Think she's got a little crush on you. Expect you're used to that.

SOPHIA. My hand is shaking.

HELEN. Oh.

SOPHIA. It will not stop.

HELEN. I'm not surprised. You had an awful shock. Here – why don't you sit?

SOPHIA *shakes her head.*

SOPHIA. I am fine.

HELEN *stops, uncertain.*

SOPHIA *glances at the window.*

…When I was a young model on photoshoot, they made me stand in the snow in a bikini. The photographer threw paint.

HELEN. Paint! Why on earth –

SOPHIA. To get a good shot. For the editor.

HELEN. Oh.

HELEN *thinks.*

Well when I was a young freelancer, you had to sit in pubs and have your breasts fondled to get a good shot at *being* the editor so...

SOPHIA *seems confused.*

Sorry, that probably doesn't make you feel better.

SOPHIA *looks down at her blood-soaked clothes again.*

SOPHIA. At least the people who do this have a purpose.

HELEN (*surprised*). Well –

SOPHIA. They are trying to frighten my husband. But they will not succeed. Our country has the right to defend itself.

Beat.

HELEN *shifts, uncomfortable.*

HELEN. ...Would you like some tea or something?

SOPHIA. No. Thank you.

HELEN. Something for your hands? The – shaking.

SOPHIA. It is just because of the speech.

HELEN. Speech?

SOPHIA. For the Women's Forum.

HELEN (*remembering*). Oh God, yes – I'd totally forgotten about that.

SOPHIA. I do not like this public speaking. It makes me very nervous.

HELEN. *That's* why you're shaking? Just say you won't do it.

SOPHIA *looks up.*

SOPHIA. ...What do you mean?

HELEN. Given the circumstances, I don't see why you should do it.

SOPHIA. The event is in less than two hours.

HELEN. So? You've had a traumatic day. And frankly you know even if – *that* hadn't happened... is it really that appropriate for us to be at a women's dinner? Tonight? Of all nights – I mean aren't there more important things going on right now, down this very hall –

SOPHIA. You don't think the women are important?

HELEN. No of course. *Of course* I think – women are important. But these women are business owners, entrepreneurs, most of them are billionaires – I mean they're not *the* most important thing going right now, are they?

SOPHIA. I think it is important to keep to your word.

HELEN (*frustrated*). Yes, of course it is. And I'm sure you've written a wonderful speech. I'm sure it's very inspiring and just what the world needs right now. What's it about?

SOPHIA. Nutrition.

HELEN. Okay.

   HELEN *turns away, barely able to be polite any more.*

SOPHIA. You think this is a foolish subject?

HELEN. Not at all.

SOPHIA. I say this too but they think it's best. They do not want it to become too – political.

   HELEN *laughs, hollow.*

HELEN. Sorry.

   She tries to contain it.

   I'm sorry.

   SOPHIA *seems offended.*

SOPHIA. I did not write this speech.

HELEN. Of course you didn't.

SOPHIA (*hurt*). I am not politician.

HELEN. No.

SOPHIA. Do you write your own speeches?

HELEN. I – *do* but –

SOPHIA. And some of your husband's too, yes?

HELEN *looks up, sharp*.

HELEN. Sorry?

SOPHIA. You were very helpful to him in his last election, this is what they say.

HELEN. Well, they say all sorts of things, don't they.

HELEN *quickly moves on*.

Anyway it's easier for me, English isn't your first language.

SOPHIA. French is not yours.

Beat.

HELEN. Well surely they've given you some training?

SOPHIA. Training?

HELEN. Media training, public speaking –

SOPHIA. Yes, of course. Hours and hours of training. I think this is why I feel so nervous – trying to remember all the things they tell me. Don't cross your arms.

HELEN. No.

SOPHIA. Smile often.

HELEN. Yes.

SOPHIA. If you make joke against your husband, put hand on his arm.

HELEN. Put hand *where*?

SOPHIA. Like this…

SOPHIA *puts a hand on* HELEN*'s arm*.

To reassure the people that you do not mean it.

HELEN. Ah /

SOPHIA. That you are not – mocking.

HELEN. No, expect he doesn't like mocking, your husband.

SOPHIA. He is very religious.

HELEN. So we hear.

SOPHIA. Religious people are not so humorous. Your husband is not religious?

HELEN. No. He's. It's not a – thing here, really.

SOPHIA. But still my husband admires him. He says that for a man so young he has strong principles.

HELEN. Yes.

SOPHIA. Even if they are wrong.

HELEN *smiles tightly, and turns away.*

It is nice to see an older woman with a younger man.

HELEN. Pardon?

SOPHIA. My mother was older than my father.

HELEN. Oh. Okay.

SOPHIA. But only by five years. Yours is much bigger gap, yes?

HELEN. Not much bigger than yours I believe, but because I'm a woman it's always a talking point.

SOPHIA. Which is unfair.

HELEN. Hmmn.

SOPHIA. But then so much of life is unfair to women.

HELEN. Depends how you look at it really.

SOPHIA. You don't think?

HELEN. I think women should be wary of victimhood. It's disempowering. I mean sure – 'call men out' if it makes you feel better, but does it actually change anything? Really? What happened to a good old-fashioned knee in the balls, you know?

SOPHIA. Knee in the balls?

HELEN. When a man crosses the line.

SOPHIA (*impressed*). You have done this?

HELEN. My day, you didn't get a choice.

SOPHIA. When they fondle your – breasts in public?

HELEN. Damn right. And never regretted it.

SOPHIA. And these men they still make you an editor?

HELEN. Well, no.

> HELEN *smiles, conceding*.

> No, not that time they didn't. Though I do think there was a grudging respect.

> SOPHIA *smiles*.

SOPHIA. It must be great asset to your husband. To have a wife so well connected in media and politics.

HELEN. Well, that was a long time ago.

SOPHIA. And he takes you to his meetings.

HELEN. Meetings?

SOPHIA. I heard that he –

HELEN. No. That's. Well… Are you sure I can't tempt you in a drink?

> SOPHIA *shakes her head*.

> Think I'm going to. Have to get through this night somehow.

> SOPHIA *watches as* HELEN *makes herself a drink*.

SOPHIA.…I hope I did not offend you with what I said before?

HELEN. What did you say before?

SOPHIA. That our country has the right to defend itself.

> HELEN *swallows, surprised*.

HELEN. No. No, of course not. Of course your country – your *adopted* country – has the right to defend itself, of course it does. In the right circumstances –

SOPHIA. And you do not think that these are the right circumstances?

HELEN. I /

SOPHIA. Despite the fact we were attacked less than two weeks ago.

HELEN. Well /

SOPHIA. Five cities, five coordinated bombings.

HELEN. Yes /

SOPHIA. Thousands killed.

HELEN. A – thousand were killed, yes /

SOPHIA. The biggest since 9–11.

HELEN. And it's appalling. It's absolutely monstrous. No one's disputing that. The whole world stands with you in sympathy.

SOPHIA. Not the whole world.

HELEN. Well, the reasonable parts.

SOPHIA. ...But?

HELEN *tries to tread carefully.*

HELEN. *But...* I'm just not sure that an – invasion or – or strikes or whatever it is they're – proposing is... the right way forward. That's all.

SOPHIA. And your husband does not believe so either?

HELEN. My husband's been very clear on his position. But look, it really doesn't matter what I think.

SOPHIA. I think it matters.

HELEN. No, the important thing is what happens in that room down the hall. What *is* happening in that room down the hall – which reminds me, where the hell is Georges?

HELEN *goes to her bag, takes out her phone.*

SOPHIA *keeps watching her.*

SOPHIA. And what do you hope is happening in that room down the hall?

HELEN *starts texting.*

HELEN. I hope that they are talking and listening.

SOPHIA. To whom?

HELEN. To everyone. I hope everyone's view is heard and everyone gets a chance to speak –

SOPHIA. And then what?

HELEN. And then... (*Carefully.*) what will be, will be.

HELEN *smiles, trying to soften it.*

SANDY *comes in – a Prada bag in one hand, phone in the other.*

SANDY. Okay, ladies, good news and bad news. Good news – cars are on their way, there's a small delay rerouting for security –

She glances out the window –

– but we're working on those protesters. (*To* SOPHIA.) Oh and the Worldwide Women's Forum are psyched you're still coming despite the earlier ordeal.

SOPHIA. They have seen the film?

SANDY. Everyone's seen the film, it's gone viral, you're a hero, you should read the tweets.

SOPHIA *reaches for her phone.*

SOPHIA. Can I read them?

SANDY. Not a good idea. You know there's always some crazy, 'she's a whore' blah blah blah.

HELEN (*disbelief*). And the bad news?

SANDY *glances at* HELEN, *sensing a 'tone'.*

Then she holds out the bag to SOPHIA.

SANDY....it's black.

Beat.

I know, I know. Not the optics we wanted.

SOPHIA *looks at the bag.*

SOPHIA. My husband will not be pleased.

SANDY. But they got it here quick – and if you think about it there's a really interesting sartorial narrative here. You know the hope and the optimism of the pastel as we started out the day, only for that dream to be cruelly shattered and – bloodsplattered by some insane fanatic, leading to the inevitable period of mourning for a world that's irreparably torn apart.

HELEN. My god.

SANDY. So we're going with that.

HELEN *heads for the door.*

HELEN. I need to speak to Georges.

SANDY *stops her.*

SANDY. You can't go out there.

HELEN. Sorry?

SANDY. We're on a lockdown. You'll need to stay in here. Just for now.

HELEN. Lockdown? That's ridiculous. Does my husband know?

SANDY. Came from the top.

HELEN*'s stunned. She points at* SOPHIA.

HELEN. But she needs a shower.

SANDY. We're working on that.

SOPHIA. I don't need a shower.

SANDY. Oh, I think you do.

SOPHIA. They can send hot water and some soap. It will be fine.

SANDY. Really? /

HELEN. Really?

SOPHIA *shrugs.*

SOPHIA. Of course.

SANDY (*to* HELEN). She's so iron curtain, I love it (*To* SOPHIA.) That'll definitely speed things up.

SANDY *heads for the door,* HELEN *follows.*

HELEN. I really need to speak to my press officer. We have
a separate announcement tomorrow – it's very important.

SANDY. So give him a call.

HELEN. I don't want to give him a call if he's just down
the hall.

SANDY. Look it's not *our* security that screwed up today, okay.
I'm doing the job of like ten people here. Sorry if there are
repercussions, but it's for your own good.

HELEN *backs off, as* SANDY *looks at* SOPHIA.

(*To* SOPHIA.) I'll find the girl, send her up with some soap.

SANDY *goes.*

HELEN *paces, irritated.*

HELEN. ...Do you like her?

SOPHIA. She is angry with me.

HELEN. How can you tell?

SOPHIA. I asked my security guard to walk ahead. He did not
see the people had got so close.

HELEN. Well I'm sure he's been suitably dealt with – she's
probably brought back the guillotine.

SOPHIA *picks up her small clutch bag and puts it on
the table.*

HELEN *starts composing an email on her phone.*

But out of the corner of her eye, she can't help watching as
SOPHIA *starts to systematically take things out of her bag
and lay them on the coffee table.*

*A key. A make-up compact. An emery board. A hand
sanitiser. A hairbrush. Some mints.*

HELEN *stares, amazed.*

...God, it's like a magician's box.

SOPHIA. Sorry?

HELEN. Your handbag. Can't even get a book into mine. Not even a small one. Not even – poetry or something.

SOPHIA. I have never tried to get a book into this.

HELEN. No.

SOPHIA. But it fits most things.

SOPHIA *pulls out a bottle of Chanel No. 5, puts it on the table.*

HELEN (*brightly*). Chanel No. 5. Only thing Marilyn Monroe wore to bed.

SOPHIA. Is it true?

HELEN. Apparently.

SOPHIA *looks at the bottle.*

SOPHIA. My mother, she loves this perfume. My auntie smuggled a bottle to Zagreb as a gift for her thirtieth birthday. We were never allowed to touch. When it was empty she filled it with water, put it on every day.

HELEN. The power of advertising.

SOPHIA. The power of the West.

Beat.

When I came to US first, I send back many bottles of this. Hundreds of bottles of Chanel No. 5. But my mother, she still uses the one with water.

HELEN. Must have sentimental value.

SOPHIA. My mother believes an intelligent woman does not leave the house without lipstick.

SOPHIA *kicks off her shoes and starts casually undressing.*

HELEN, *slightly bemused, looks at the bottle.*

HELEN. You know I must confess I've never quite got the big deal about Chanel No. 5. To me it's always just smelled a bit like – old ladies.

SOPHIA. Old ladies?

HELEN. I mean not on you of course. Or your mother. And it's a very pretty bottle I can appreciate that, it's just –

HELEN *picks it up.*

SOPHIA *looks up and suddenly shouts –*

SOPHIA. No no don't touch!

HELEN. I /

SOPHIA (*urgent*). Put it down at once.

HELEN *freezes.*

Put it down *at once*!

HELEN *quickly puts the bottle down.*

SOPHIA *takes it and moves it towards herself protectively.*

HELEN (*shocked*). Sorry I…

SOPHIA. I did not mean to startle you.

HELEN. No no it's –

SOPHIA. I am not being rude.

HELEN.…perfume's a very – personal thing.

SOPHIA *continues to get undressed.*

A long beat.

…Have I –

SOPHIA. Can you help with this, please?

SOPHIA *gestures to the zip on the back of her dress.*

HELEN. Oh…Yes. Of course.

SOPHIA *comes towards her, turns around.*

HELEN, *a little rattled, pulls down her zip.*

SOPHIA. Thank you.

A long silence as SOPHIA *wriggles out of her dress and stands in her underwear/slip.*

She starts folding her clothes neatly and putting them on the chair.

HELEN, *trying to distract herself, goes back to her phone, continues tapping out an email.*

Eventually –

…it is not perfume.

HELEN *looks up.*

HELEN. Hmnn?

SOPHIA. In the bottle. It is not perfume.

HELEN *glances at the bottle.*

HELEN.…what is it?

SOPHIA *considers.*

Then –

SOPHIA.…Poison.

HELEN. *Poison?*

SOPHIA *nods.*

HELEN *looks at the bottle again, smiles.*

You're joking.

SOPHIA. It is in case something happens. A kidnapping, an ambush…

HELEN. You have – poison in a bottle in case of an ambush?

SOPHIA. You don't carry something?

HELEN.…Not like that I don't.

SOPHIA. This surprises me. The world is a dangerous place now. I would rather be ready than sorry.

HELEN. I'm sorry, I'm supposed to believe that – *that's* poison in that bottle?

SOPHIA. That is what I said.

Beat.

HELEN.…what kind?

SOPHIA. They do not tell me this.

HELEN. Novichok? Cyanide?

SOPHIA. They do not say.

HELEN. I see.

SOPHIA *looks at her.*

SOPHIA. You do not believe me?

HELEN. Well it's hard to believe.

HELEN *sceptically leans down for a closer look.*

What does it do?

SOPHIA. It does what poison is supposed to do.

HELEN. And what are *you* supposed to do with it?

SOPHIA. It depends what is required. If things get really bad, I am to drink it.

HELEN *laughs.*

HELEN. Oh come on…

SOPHIA *looks up, deadly serious.*

SOPHIA. Only if things get really bad.

HELEN. And this is just – fine with you, is it? Carrying – poison around in your purse?

SOPHIA. You read the newspapers in my country.

HELEN. Yes but –

SOPHIA. And Europe is having attacks every month.

HELEN. Well not quite every –

SOPHIA. Paris, Berlin, Rome –

HELEN. I know /

SOPHIA. Every major European city /

HELEN. I'm aware of what's been going on.

SOPHIA. These are turbulent times. Our lives are under threat.

HELEN *stops, studying her.*

HELEN. Well... I can certainly appreciate there might be some concern that – *yours* is under threat. But me –

SOPHIA. Because your husband is pacifist?

HELEN. Because my husband is – a different sort of figure, yes.

SOPHIA. So you do not believe his policies make you vulnerable?

HELEN. His enemies would certainly like us to think so, but no, I don't.

SOPHIA. He has allowed many people to come here.

HELEN. And *none* have been connected to any attacks.

SOPHIA. So you do not believe that as the wife of a president your life could be in danger?

HELEN. I mean it's always a possibility... And I'm not saying people shouldn't take precautions, but this seems a little... paranoid.

SOPHIA. Not to me.

HELEN *takes this in*.

HELEN. Well forgive my naiveté. But I doubt things will ever get so bad here that my security team will start concocting little bottles of Chanel No. 5 –

SOPHIA. Security team?

HELEN. CIA, Secret Service, whoever's given you that stuff – God.

SOPHIA. I did not say it was the secret service. Or the CIA.

HELEN *stops*.

HELEN. Well who gave to you?

Beat.

SOPHIA. Friends.

HELEN. *Friends?*

SOPHIA. Old friends. Who like to help.

HELEN *frowns.*

HELEN. So your – people… don't know you have this?

SOPHIA. Presidents have been shot and killed in the country
  I now live in. If the Secret Service cannot protect them, why
  should I trust they can protect me?

HELEN.…What about your husband?

  SOPHIA *doesn't answer.*

  HELEN *glances back at the bottle, a lot less certain now.*

  …Don't you feel nervous carrying that around?

SOPHIA. Why?

HELEN. What if it – spilled or something?

SOPHIA. Then I would be dead.

HELEN. And that doesn't scare you?

SOPHIA. Actually it makes me feel safe. I like to know that if
  anything happens. Anything truly terrible. I will be the one
  in control.

  A knock on the door and GEORGES *enters, breathless,
  apologetic.*

GEORGES (*to* HELEN). I am so sorry it is completely crazy
  here –

  He sees SOPHIA *in her slip, jumps and covers his eyes.*

  Oh, madame! I did not realise –

SOPHIA. It's okay.

  He turns quickly, embarrassed

GEORGES. I'm so sorry. I will go.

SOPHIA. Many people in your country have seen me in less.

HELEN (*under her breath*). True.

GEORGES (*mortified*). My apologies.

HELEN. Are we still being kept prisoner?

GEORGES. It will not be for much longer. It just keeps... some people happy.

HELEN *makes a face at him*.

HELEN. I've been emailing.

GEORGES. Yes I received them, but there are so many people – media, diplomats – and with the updates from the meeting –

HELEN*'s head comes up, sharp*.

HELEN. What updates?

GEORGES *glances at* SOPHIA, *careful*.

GEORGES. Things are going well.

HELEN. You've spoken to him?

GEORGES. To his secretary, yes.

HELEN. So when will he sign off on the press release?

GEORGES. I don't know, madame. There are a lot of important things –

HELEN. *This* is an important thing, Georges.

GEORGES. Yes I know. /

The CATERING ASSISTANT *comes to the door with a simple bucket and some soap*.

CATERING ASSISTANT (*uncertain*). Quelqu'un a demandé du savon et de l'eau?

GEORGES *turns*.

GEORGES (*to the* CATERING ASSISTANT). Qu'est-ce que c'est?

The CATERING ASSISTANT *nervously gestures to* SOPHIA.

CATERING ASSISTANT....Je pense que c'est pour elle.

GEORGES *rushes to the* CATERING ASSISTANT *appalled*.

GEORGES. Non non non non non. Ce n'est pas possible. C'est la femme du Président.

SOPHIA. It is fine. I asked for it.

GEORGES (*to* SOPHIA). Oh no, madame. We cannot /

SOPHIA. Bring it here.

> *The* CATERING ASSISTANT *walks over to* SOPHIA.
>
> SOPHIA *quite perfunctorily takes the bucket off her.*
>
> *She picks up the towel and dips it in the water and starts washing herself.*

GEORGES (*appalled*). This cannot happen –

HELEN. She asked for it. (*To* GEORGES, *frustrated.*) Can I just have a quick word?

GEORGES. This is not how we do things –

SOPHIA. It is not a problem.

GEORGES. Madame, you are a First Lady / we are the hosts –

HELEN. You know I am starting to feel decidedly invisible here, Georges – *What is going on?*

> GEORGES *stops, surprised.*

GEORGES. …Nothing, madame. We are a little behind, that's all.

HELEN. Behind?

GEORGES. With the schedule.

HELEN (*voice rising*). I don't care about the schedule!

> SOPHIA *and the* CATERING ASSISTANT *look up.*
>
> HELEN *feels slightly exposed but she is not backing down.*

Are we all still on the same page, Georges?

GEORGES. …yes, madame.

HELEN. So can you somehow get a message to my husband that I would like to speak with him as soon as possible?

GEORGES. He knows, madame. I am sure when the meeting breaks he will want to speak with you too.

HELEN. And when will that be?

GEORGES. Not for a few hours. You can go to the dinner and back.

HELEN *groans*.

(*To* SOPHIA.) The drive to Nice is forty-five minutes, maybe a little longer with the snow –

HELEN. And when are we allowed out of this room?

GEORGES. I will check.

He starts to go.

HELEN *suddenly feels anxious.*

HELEN. Well don't take forever. I know we're not the most important thing on your minds. We're just wives. With tiny handbags and big husbands...

GEORGES (*to* SOPHIA). This is her sense of humour, take no notice.

GEORGES *spots the Chanel on the table*

Ah Chanel numéro 5... pour la femme élégante.

SOPHIA *smiles*. GEORGES *smiles back, delighted.*

The CATERING ASSISTANT *reaches over with a towel and tries to help* SOPHIA.

(*To the girl, curt.*) Vous, venez avec moi!

The CATERING ASSISTANT *scurries out after him.*

The two women are left alone.

SOPHIA *carries on cleaning herself.*

HELEN *stares out the window, distracted.*

SOPHIA. I think you would like to be in this meeting down the hall, yes?

HELEN. Wouldn't you?

SOPHIA. Are you worried?

HELEN *turns.*

HELEN. Worried?

SOPHIA. For your husband.

HELEN. Not at all.

SOPHIA. He was very young when you met him, yes?

HELEN. He was – *younger.*

SOPHIA. Sixteen?

HELEN. Sixteen!

SOPHIA. Where I come from fifteen is a man.

HELEN. Well where I come from it's a criminal offence. And he was seventeen alright when we met. Eighteen by the time we actually – you mustn't believe everything you – and *he* pursued *me* alright? He's very headstrong like that.

SOPHIA. Of course. He is President. Of Europe now, they say.

HELEN *turns away, annoyed.*

SOPHIA *continues cleaning herself.*

My husband was already successful lawyer when I met him. He had given up alcohol, was running for Governor.

HELEN. Had he found God yet?

SOPHIA. Oh yes. The first time, before we make love, he prayed.

HELEN. He… wow.

SOPHIA. But sometimes I wonder what it would have been like. To know him as a boy.

HELEN *takes a breath, decides not to take it on.*

Maybe he'd still be idealist, like your husband.

HELEN. My husband's more pragmatic than you think.

SOPHIA. So he might make deal?

HELEN. You know, I don't think we should be talking about this.

SOPHIA. The world is standing on a precipice.

HELEN. I'm well aware of that.

SOPHIA. But my husband did not have to consult anyone.

HELEN.…I'm sorry?

SOPHIA. He did not have to come here and take this meeting.
He did not have to accept your husband's invitation, engage
in these talks –

HELEN. I think you'll find he did.

SOPHIA. No. He could have just gone ahead with it.

HELEN. No.

SOPHIA. No?

HELEN. No – alright, we are talking about this, are we? Fine.
Okay… Yes, *technically* he could have just gone ahead with
it. Pushed his – button or whatever, broken international law
and he hasn't, and given that he's barely been in power six
months, we're all very grateful for that. But just because he's
agreed to come here does give not him an excuse –

SOPHIA. You call one thousand people's death an excuse?

HELEN. I'm – sorry if that sounded glib… but what happened
in your country was just a criminal attack, by a terrorist cell.

SOPHIA. Who have found safehouse with a cruel regime.

HELEN. That may be so. But we've been down this road
before. You bomb them, they'll regroup. In a few years,
they'll come back stronger, better, meanwhile, you've started
a war with a country whose allies have nuclear weapons.

SOPHIA. A country that kills and tortures their own people.

HELEN. We have to learn from history. There are other ways.

SOPHIA. Like sending the UN?

HELEN. Yes, for starters.

SOPHIA (*dry*). Because that worked so well in Srebrenica.

HELEN*'s taken aback.*

HELEN. Their allies have been very clear. If your husband goes
ahead with this, the reprisals will be severe.

SOPHIA. My husband does not want a nuclear war.

HELEN. But it could lead very easily to it. That part of the
world. A strike, a retaliation – boom.

SOPHIA. And what if it was your daughter?

HELEN. My daughter?

SOPHIA. Killed in the attack. You have children, yes?

HELEN. Well *children* – my daughter's nearly forty. But you know, frankly I find those sorts of comparisons utterly meaningless. What – only a parent can understand the true impact of a tragedy? Nonsense. Anyone with an ounce of empathy can understand it. As a mother I do not believe myself morally superior to a woman who's not. Or a – trans person who's not, or anyone who's not for that matter.

SOPHIA. I am not.

HELEN (*faltering*). Right. Yes exactly…

SOPHIA. But if I *were* a mother, I would want justice.

HELEN. No, you would want revenge.

SOPHIA. It is not the same thing?

HELEN. Absolutely not. The only thing – *this* can possibly achieve, is to make the world an even more dangerous place.

Beat.

SOPHIA.…. And what if your husband agrees with my husband?

HELEN. He won't.

SOPHIA. The people in your country are angry. They too have suffered attacks.

HELEN. Of different kinds. You talk about them like they're all the same, but they're not. You know it might not be convenient for some of the leaders in that room, but on this continent there have been as many far-right lunatics walking into mosques and opening fire as any kind of –

SOPHIA. People don't care about the details.

HELEN. But the details matter.

SOPHIA. They just want it to stop. Your husband has failed them.

HELEN. Not true.

SOPHIA. He promises jobs, he gives them to immigrants.

HELEN. Are we supposed to starve them?

SOPHIA. He is plummeting in polls. They say he is weak.

HELEN. I think the people outside that window would disagree.

SOPHIA. Are they the majority?

HELEN *falters*.

HELEN. ...My husband is a man of great integrity. Who has spent the last four years doing things a different way. He will not be cowed.

SOPHIA *puts her towel down and looks at* HELEN.

SOPHIA. So you trust your husband?

HELEN. Implicitly. Why – don't you trust yours?

SOPHIA. ...No.

Beat.

And he hasn't even got anyone pregnant.

HELEN *is blindsided*.

...I read the papers in your country too.

Beat.

HELEN (*quietly*). That's – not in the papers.

SOPHIA. Yet.

A very long silence.

HELEN. ...I see.

Beat.

I see.

She looks at SOPHIA.

So this was – calculated, was it?

SOPHIA. How do you mean?

HELEN. You, me, this room. You armed with your little piece of – information.

SOPHIA. No.

HELEN. Are you behind this 'lockdown' too?

SOPHIA. Of course not. We are in your country.

SOPHIA *opens the Prada bag, takes out the dress.*

HELEN *watches as she steps into it.*

HELEN. ...Does everyone know?

SOPHIA. Everyone?

SOPHIA *pulls up the dress.*

HELEN. Your husband, your – people, everyone.

SOPHIA. How else do you think I find out?

HELEN *closes her eyes.*

...It must be very painful. To be betrayed like this.

HELEN *opens her eyes.*

A man you trust. A man you love. A man you have helped –

HELEN *looks at* SOPHIA *with pure hate.*

HELEN. What do you want?

SOPHIA. ...Excuse me?

HELEN. What. Do you. Want.

SOPHIA *doesn't answer.*

Is this some kind of – strategy or something? To – bully me, bully my husband. Strong-arm us into agreeing with you? Well I'm sorry but you're too late. We're announcing it tomorrow.

SOPHIA (*surprised*). Tomorrow?

HELEN. Yes, imagine that's really ruined it for you.

SOPHIA. And you think this is a good idea? With everything else?

HELEN (*disbelief*). Are you trying to advise me?

SOPHIA. I am simply concerned.

HELEN. Oh that's really lovely of you. (*Vicious*.) So I'll ask again – what do you want?

The door opens and SANDY *and* GEORGES *walk in.*

SANDY. Finally! Things are moving. /

GEORGES. The cars have arrived. /

HELEN *moves quickly to the window as* SANDY *sees* SOPHIA –

SANDY. Look at you! Oh *yes,* that is gonna *work.*

GEORGES. The black is sensational, madame.

SANDY *briefly adjusts* SOPHIA*'s dress.*

SANDY. Everything's sensational on this one. So we'll do your make-up in the car, tweak this hair –

SOPHIA *picks up the bag.*

SOPHIA. I do not think the bag – [goes.]

SANDY. Don't worry about the bag. No one's looking at that. They'll be looking at you, thinking wow what a pair of balls. Only a few hours ago she was under attack /

GEORGES (*to* SOPHIA) You look wonderful, madame – Hélène, are you ready?

As SOPHIA *and* SANDY *move towards the door,* SANDY *brushing* SOPHIA*'s dress.*

SANDY (*to* SOPHIA). Trust me, they're gonna eat this up.

GEORGES (*calling*). Hélène, we are going…

HELEN *hasn't moved.*

He looks at her concerned.

…Hélène?

HELEN. I'm not coming.

Everybody stops.

SANDY.…What?

GEORGES (*shocked*). What do you mean?

HELEN *turns*.

HELEN. I mean I'm not coming. To the dinner.

SANDY *looks at* GEORGES.

GEORGES. But you must.

HELEN. Why? I'm not making a speech. The First Lady's the – hero of the hour. Let her have her moment.

SANDY. Oh come on, it's not a competition.

HELEN. I'm not competing.

SANDY. People love you both, okay.

GEORGES (*firm*). Hélène, you are their guest. We are the host country.

HELEN. I'm not leaving this room, Georges.

SANDY. Two minutes ago you couldn't wait to get out.

HELEN. Well now I'm staging my own little sit-in. Like those people outside with the placards.

GEORGES. Hélène, please consider our position. The President will want you at the dinner.

HELEN (*firm*). I'm not setting foot outside that door, Georges, until the meeting breaks.

GEORGES *loses his temper*.

GEORGES. And what are we supposed to tell the forum, hmmn? What are we supposed to tell the press?

SANDY (*tapping on her phone*). I know what we'll be telling them.

HELEN. Is that a threat?

Suddenly SOPHIA *swoons*.

SOPHIA. Oh my – [goodness.]

GEORGES. Madame!

GEORGES *rushes to her*.

SANDY. What happened? Is she okay?

SOPHIA. I need to… sit.

GEORGES. Please /

> GEORGES *helps* SOPHIA *to a chair.*

SANDY. Are you alright? / Is she alright?

SOPHIA. I do not feel well.

> *As* SANDY *and* GEORGES *gather round,* HELEN *watches her, suspicious.*

SANDY. Do we need a doctor?

SOPHIA. Maybe.

SANDY. Okay.

> SANDY *picks up her phone.*
>
> SOPHIA *stops her.*

SOPHIA. But not yet.

> *Beat.*

…I do not think I should go to this dinner.

SANDY. What?

HELEN (*alarmed*). What?

SOPHIA. I will stay here with Hélène.

HELEN. No.

SOPHIA. It is best.

HELEN. There's no need for that.

SANDY. Okay, *what* is going on here, ladies?

> *The two ladies look at one another.*

SOPHIA. If Hélène does not go to the dinner, I do not go either.

GEORGES. I think it's better if you both go –

HELEN. It's just the Women's Forum.

GEORGES (*losing temper*). No it is *the world*. The world is watching and we are allies. We need to present a united front.

SOPHIA. I agree. We will both stay here.

SANDY. Look, we're *really* behind, okay. All you gotta do is show up, eat some – clams, read the speech and come back to the hotel. It's not that difficult, *I* could do it if I had the clothes.

The two women stay silent, implacable.

…What are we supposed to tell them?

SOPHIA. Tell them… tell them that after events of today, the President's wife and I have decided to wait.

SANDY. For *what*?

SOPHIA. In solidarity.

HELEN. Solidarity!

SOPHIA. With the people. Those who support my husband and those who support yours.

HELEN *laughs, hollow.*

HELEN. Oh please.

SANDY. So what, this is some kind of – vigil? For peace?

SANDY *looks at* GEORGES.

Can we do something with that?

GEORGES. This is not a good idea, Hélène, I must insist –

SOPHIA. And we would like to be left alone.

GEORGES (*surprised*). Pardon?

SOPHIA. The President's wife and I need some privacy.

HELEN. No we don't.

SOPHIA. I think we do /

HELEN. We absolutely don't.

SANDY. Okay, you know what? We're gonna just give you some space.

HELEN. We don't need / space –

SANDY (*to* SOPHIA). You're not feeling well – (*To* HELEN.)
    You're not feeling well. It's been a rough day, I get it –
    Georges?

She nods for him to follow her to the door.

HELEN. Where are you going?

SANDY. We'll figure something out – *Georges*?

HELEN. Georges!

GEORGES (*angry*). Vous rendez les choses très difficiles,
    Hélène.

He walks off muttering to himself.

Putain de merde.

He goes. The two ladies are alone again.

SOPHIA *looks at* HELEN.

HELEN *looks away*.

A silence.

SOPHIA. She is –

HELEN *puts up her hand*.

HELEN. Don't.

SOPHIA. I am simply –

HELEN. Just. Don't.

HELEN *paces*.

SOPHIA *watches*.

SOPHIA. …She is member of your husband's cabinet, this
    woman, yes?

HELEN *stops*.

This must be difficult. A pornographic film star or – even an
    actress, one can always look down on. But a woman with
    education and political class similar to oneself…

HELEN *simmers*.

This is not so easy. No?

Beat.

HELEN. Do you think much about why your husband didn't marry until so late?

Beat.

Why he waited till he was running for Governor, why he – prays so much? Do you think about that a lot?

SOPHIA. Not really.

HELEN. No. I wouldn't either if I were you.

HELEN *starts to pace again.*

SOPHIA. You think that I am trying to hurt you.

HELEN. I don't know what you're trying to do.

SOPHIA. I am not, believe me. People say things about both our husbands. That yours is – puppet whose wife pulls strings, that mine –

HELEN. Fucks men?

SOPHIA *stops.*

I mean don't get me wrong I don't have a problem with him fucking men. It's just his policies have so consistently fucked the men who want to fuck men – or marry them for that matter. But then your husband has never had a problem with hypocrisy. He locks up immigrants, yet he's married to you.

Beat.

SOPHIA. I can see that you are angry. This was not my intention –

HELEN. I've no interest in *what was your intention.*

SOPHIA. I had hoped we could be friends.

HELEN *stares at her, incredulous.*

Is your daughter as passionate as you?

HELEN. Can we just stop this, please. Before somebody says something they truly regret.

SOPHIA. Like what?

HELEN. Like why don't you have your own children, if you're so obsessed. One of your husband's special interests is what women do with their wombs – why doesn't he do something with yours?

For the first time SOPHIA *looks hurt.*

SOPHIA. This is a sensitive subject.

HELEN. Well there you are, you see, we've finally crossed a line.

SOPHIA. I would have liked very much to have children.

HELEN. You don't need to explain, I was making a point.

SOPHIA. My husband too, would have liked it. But I cannot.

Beat.

HELEN (*cold*). Well I'm sorry about that.

SOPHIA *looks at her.*

SOPHIA. I mean I *will* not.

HELEN *looks up surprised.*

It would not be responsible for me to bring a child into this world.

HELEN *glances at her, uncertain.*

HELEN. ...Well at this moment in time I'd have to agree with you.

SOPHIA. It has nothing to do with a war.

Beat.

I don't trust men... I worry if I had a child and he was a boy, I would be unable to love him.

HELEN *is taken aback, despite herself.*

HELEN. That's ridiculous. Of course you'd be able to love him. Of course you would, you don't even think about it.

SOPHIA. I know what men are capable of.

HELEN. Don't we *all* know what they're capable of.

SOPHIA. I don't believe so.

HELEN. Yes we do. They start wars, they colonise things, they cheat on their wives – men're awful, we know. Only trouble is, women are capable of just as much.

SOPHIA. I did not say women are always to be trusted.

HELEN. No, I don't see how *you* could.

SOPHIA. But men are what I know.

HELEN looks at her, sensing something.

She decides to pursue.

HELEN. Well you're going to have to offer up something a bit more concrete I'm afraid…

SOPHIA. Concrete.

HELEN. Specific. Cos this is all getting a bit too generalised for me.

SOPHIA. Ah yes. Journalist.

SOPHIA looks at her, considering.

Then –

…Very well.

HELEN folds her arms ready to listen.

When I was fifteen years old, my mother sent me to stay with a cousin, who lived in small town in the countryside. She was unwell, my mother. There were too many children. She wanted me out of her hair.

HELEN. Okay…

SOPHIA. This town was on the coast. Beautiful part of the country, I loved it there. I could stay out late at night in the village. Many evenings I would sit on the wall with the local kids and swing my legs and wear my American jeans. And – I got attention. Which I liked.

And this cousin, she had a boyfriend. He would come over some nights to play cards. He was political, and passionate, and always talking about the things that were happening in the country that people did not realise were happening. And when my mother's cousin was out of the room, he would let me have sip of his vodka. Or beer. And he would ask how many boyfriends I have in the village and how many hearts I have broken…

She smiles.

I liked this man.

And then one night, five or six weeks maybe, into my stay, he comes to the house with three friends and says to my mother's cousin they will take me for a drive. It was late, but my mother's cousin did not object. And I did not object either. Because as I said, I liked him.

So I went to the van with the boyfriend and the three men and they drive me up to some hills. And they are laughing and talking and all I can see from inside the car is blackness and the shapes of trees going by very fast. And I realise I don't see any houses, there are no houses where we are driving. And this van is moving very quickly, and the men keep looking back at me and suddenly, I start to feel afraid. And I ask one, the one I know, the boyfriend of my mother's cousin, to take me back to the house. I don't like this drive any more I say. And he says I am being stupid and they are taking me to party. But I keep saying I don't like it, I want to get out and I get more and more upset until eventually I am screaming.

So they stop the car.

And they tell me to be quiet.

And the man sitting next to me – a man I do not know – he leans very close and he tells me to lie down. I do not. So he calls another one and *he* gets into the back seat and the two of them they push me down. And one of them gets on top of me and unbuttons my jeans and drags my underwear down to my knees and when I struggle he shoves his fist inside me and tells me to shut up or he will do it again. And he laughs. He laughs when I cry. He laughs when I piss myself, and then he swaps places with the other one. And the other one. And then the first one…

Beat.

And all the time my mother's cousin's boyfriend is standing outside the van smoking. While the three men inside do – what you can imagine.

HELEN *stares at her.*

Worse than you can imagine.

Beat.

And when it is finished, they drive me back down through the hills. And they talk to one another about politics and something someone heard on radio and whether there will really be a war. Arguing passionately, forgetting I am there. And my mother's cousin's boyfriend drops the men in the village and they give him some money. And as we drive off, one of them looks back and… he waves.

HELEN.…waves?

SOPHIA *nods.*

And then what happened?

SOPHIA. And then we go home. And my mother's cousin gives me a plate of chicken. And I eat it. And I go to bed.

HELEN.…Did you tell her what happened?

SOPHIA. She knew what happened.

Beat.

I only stayed a few more weeks, then I went home to my parents.

HELEN. And you told them?

SOPHIA *looks at her.*

SOPHIA. What?

HELEN. That those men had raped you. Viciously.

SOPHIA. There was nothing they could do.

HELEN (*growing anger*). Are you saying they just got away with it?

SOPHIA. In my country so many women were raped in Homeland War, we have a law now to pay them compensation.

HELEN. So this was the war?

SOPHIA. Just before.

HELEN. So these men were what – Serbians?

SOPHIA. They were men. Their politics is simply an excuse. They were men who wanted to send message. To let me know that my pretty face, that aroused their desire, or made them feel foolish, was not more powerful than they were. If I think I can control them by walking round village in my American jeans, they are here to tell me otherwise. If I think I can humiliate them with rejection or indifference – they are letting me know that no – no, *they* will always be able to humiliate me. *They* are the ones with the power.

Beat.

HELEN.....well not any more.

SOPHIA *looks up, surprised.*

You have – power now. You're a First Lady. You're married to the most powerful man in the – I mean your husband, if he wanted to –

SOPHIA. My husband does not know.

HELEN *stops, shocked.*

You think my country wants First Lady who's been gang-raped? They already think I am prostitute.

HELEN. That is not – true.

SOPHIA. Please. Ex-model, rich husband, Eastern Europe accent. If I was from Paris or Italy like your other first-lady ex-models, if I was aristocrat, they would never say this. But I am wrong sort of European.

HELEN. There's no – wrong sort of European.

SOPHIA. My husband was upset when I explained this. He is not well travelled. Maybe if he had known he'd make different choice of wife.

HELEN. You should not make light of what happened.

SOPHIA. I do not make light of it. I am last person who would make light of it.

HELEN. ...and you've really never told him?

SOPHIA *looks at her directly.*

SOPHIA. I have never told anyone. Except you.

HELEN *doesn't know what to do.*

HELEN. ...Why?

SOPHIA. Why?

HELEN. Why would you – tell me this?

SOPHIA. Because you asked. And because I figure if I tell you my secret...

HELEN. ...I might tell you mine?

SOPHIA. You might begin to trust me. We have more in common than you think.

Beat.

HELEN *is deeply unnerved. She tries to gather herself.*

HELEN. ...Look. That is a – dreadful story.

SOPHIA. It is not a story.

HELEN. It is a dreadful – *thing*, it is a dreadful thing to have happened and I'm sorry, I am... but I don't see what it has to do with –

SOPHIA. You are making this announcement tomorrow? About the pregnancy.

HELEN *frowns.*

HELEN. ...yes?

SOPHIA. And your husband will stand down?

HELEN. No.

Beat.

No. Why would he stand down?

SOPHIA. You think the people will put up with this?

HELEN. What's it got to do with the people?

SOPHIA. A man who cannot keep his seed in the right woman, how will he steer his country through a war.

HELEN. Well hopefully there isn't going to be a war.

Beat.

And actually, you know one of the things I most admire about this country is that they have a grown-up attitude to sex.

SOPHIA. Sex?

HELEN. Yes, sex. That's all it is, that's all it was.

SOPHIA. How do you know?

HELEN. Because he's told me.

SOPHIA. And you believe him?

HELEN. *Yes*. And believe it or not I understand. We've been married twenty years.

SOPHIA. So you have been unfaithful too?

HELEN. No – well, I was unfaithful to my first husband. I *left* my first husband *and* my child, I mean I'm certainly not one to be moralising. I understand very well what desire can do.

She looks at SOPHIA.

It doesn't have to be the end of the world.

SOPHIA. So what will you do?

HELEN. We'll – tell the truth.

SOPHIA *looks at her, curious.*

That's what we've decided. That's what I'm trying to –

SOPHIA. Talk to him about?

HELEN. He's already agreed. We drafted this press release four days ago, it's just he's spent the last forty-eight hours locked in a room with his advisers so… believe it or not, this is not the most convenient time for a war.

SOPHIA. He must be nervous. It will be difficult.

HELEN. No, I don't think it will actually. Actually, I think it will be easier. People are tired of politics... Marriages struggle. People stray. Nothing is ever black and white. An honest politician in this day and age is not one who is perfect but one who owns up to his imperfections. They say yes, I had an affair. Yes, I hurt my wife. Yes, I've made terrible mistakes and in many ways I'm a fool, but I am going to make it right. By doing my duty. Because that's what a president does. So yes, I'm having a child with someone else but I will stay in my marriage and work at that marriage and still do what is right by that child. And still do what is right by *this* country. It might be complicated and it might it be difficult, but I will do it because it's the responsible thing to do. And a good president *is* responsible, a good president *is* accountable – not only for his own actions but those of his people – and I believe, I *know* I am a good president.

SOPHIA. I think you'd be a good president too.

HELEN*'s embarrassed.*

HELEN. No I was just –

SOPHIA. It is a shame.

HELEN. The public deserve the truth. He would be the politician none of the rest of them are. If Bill Clinton had just said yes – okay, yes I fucked her, or whatever with the cigar. Yes I did have sexual relations with that woman – that *girl* – maybe everyone would just have had to man up and accept it. This is what happens, this is real life, *presidents fuck*. Deal with it.

SOPHIA. But he didn't.

HELEN. No but if he had –

SOPHIA. And they didn't. They judged him.

HELEN. His presidency survived it.

SOPHIA. But his wife's did not.

Silence.

My husband would not respect a man like this. Who confesses to his weaknesses.

HELEN. Well I've made myself clear. It's the only way I'll stand by him. And he needs me to stand by him.

SOPHIA. Of course.

HELEN. He *needs* me.

SOPHIA....It is just my experience that when men have power, they will do anything to keep it.

Beat.

My husband was very tender when I first met him. Very gentle and soft.

Beat.

I do not know if these things you say about him are true. It would not matter. People have marriages for many reasons – companionship, friendship, someone to help with household tasks. I would be happy with this kind of marriage. As you say, it is just sex.

Beat.

But now he speaks to me only in front of other people. He will only hold my hand if there are cameras. And he shouts, terrible things, whenever I make stupid mistake. It does not matter that *I* did not run for election. It does not matter that I cannot open a window, or go out into the street. It does not matter that I cannot even sit on toilet without some man with a headphone standing outside listening to me urinate –

For a moment SOPHIA's upset breaks through.

But she gathers herself.

She looks at HELEN.

These indignities do not matter to a person in power.

Beat.

And I am the one at who they throw the blood.

A knock on the door. HELEN jumps, startled.

HELEN. Come in.

GEORGES (*peering in*). Ladies, I have some news –

HELEN. Yes?

He notes the strained atmosphere.

GEORGES....Everything is alright?

HELEN. What is it?

GEORGES. We have notified the Women's Forum you will not be in attendance. They are disappointed but understand.

HELEN. That's it?

GEORGES. Uh, no. The meeting is taking a short break.

HELEN *looks up, sharp.*

HELEN. So they're out?

Something beeps on GEORGES' phone, he reads it, distracted.

GEORGES. For ten minutes or so yes... the President has requested to see you.

HELEN*'s visibly relieved.*

HELEN. Well that's – wonderful. That's fantastic. Can he come here? Or should I go down? I should probably go down if there's only / ten –

GEORGES *suddenly looks embarrassed.*

GEORGES. Oh no, madame, I'm sorry... I meant the First Lady.

He gestures to SOPHIA.

HELEN *visibly deflates.*

(*To* SOPHIA.) Your husband has requested to see you in the meeting room.

Beat.

SOPHIA....Of course.

GEORGES. Security will escort you down the hall.

SOPHIA *calmly picks up her bag and stands up.*

SOPHIA. Thank you.

> SOPHIA *glances at* HELEN, *briefly, then leaves the room.*

> GEORGES *gestures that he has to follow* –

GEORGES. I'm sorry I have just received an email –

HELEN. What about *our* President, Georges?

> GEORGES *stops.*

GEORGES. Ah yes, he has given a message.

HELEN. A message!

GEORGES. He is consulting with his ministers now but when he has finished –

HELEN. Is she here?

> GEORGES *is shocked.*

GEORGES. What? No, madame –

HELEN. Don't bullshit me, Georges.

GEORGES. I am not /

HELEN. He promised me. He *promised – is she here*?

GEORGES. He is speaking with the Minister of Defence.

HELEN (*upset*). I'm being cut out.

GEORGES. Let me see if I can talk with him.

HELEN. I'm coming with you.

> *He tries to prevent her.*

GEORGES. It is better if you stay.

HELEN. *I don't want to stay.*

GEORGES (*firm*). Do you want to undermine him?

> HELEN *stops.*

If you go down to that meeting room now, you know what they will say. At this moment in time, do you really want them thinking he is not his own man?

HELEN *backs off, wounded.*

Silence.

HELEN (*quietly*)....I would just like to see him.

Beat.

I'm worried about the press release, if we keep putting it off –

GEORGES. We are not putting it off.

HELEN. But if this story gets ahead of us –

GEORGES. I know how to do my job, Hélène. I am working on it. As soon as I have his approval, we will send it. (*Softer.*) Can you please just trust me?

Beat. HELEN *nods.*

As SANDY *enters – with various gadgets – reading something off a laptop.*

SANDY. Oh this is great, this is really great. (*To* HELEN.) You wanna hear what they're saying?

GEORGES (*to* HELEN). I will speak to him.

GEORGES goes, SANDY *continues, oblivious.*

HELEN *moves to the window, unsettled.*

SANDY. Listen to this – 'The gravity of the situation is exemplified by the sudden withdrawal of the two First Ladies from a planned dinner later this evening. The ladies, whose husbands have long had a terse relationship, have reportedly come together in an act of solidarity with the people, in the hope of strengthening the talks, averting military action and aiding the peace' – well that'll probably go to shit, but the rest is good right?

HELEN *bristles.* SANDY *leans in to the screen.*

Just wish they had a better visual instead of all that blood.

She suddenly shouts at the screen.

Hey, stop that, you little shit! I can see you.

HELEN *turns.*

HELEN. Pardon?

SANDY. Got my kid on FaceTime.

HELEN looks at the laptop.

HELEN. Oh.

SANDY. Only way I know he's doing his homework – (*To the screen, shouting.*) Oh my god – you've had enough sugar today, you hear me? (*To* HELEN, *polite.*) I'm sorry, do you mind?

HELEN. Go ahead.

SANDY puts on some headphones.

SANDY (*to the screen, angry*). You hear what I said? That's enough… Yes I can, Craig… Yes I can – I can come through that screen and kick your butt is what. Where's Grandma?… Well I'm calling her… Yes I am, I'm calling her now.

He hangs up on her.

She throws the headphones down. Starts texting.

Damnit.

Beat.

HELEN smiles, bemused.

HELEN. …How many do you have?

SANDY. Three. Seventeen, fifteen, twelve… That's twelve.

HELEN. Teenagers.

SANDY. Oh yeah.

Another of SANDY*'s phones buzzes. She picks it up.*

HELEN. Don't know how you keep track of all those gadgets.

SANDY. This one's a dating app. (*Looking.*) Gotta bite.

She looks at the phone.

(*Clicking.*) Not bad.

She shows HELEN *the picture.*

HELEN. No.

SANDY. Ever used one of these things?

HELEN....No.

SANDY. Not a bad way to meet someone.

HELEN *silently takes this in.*

Hey, is it true what they say about French men?

HELEN. I don't want to know what they say about French men.

SANDY (*laughs*). What've I gotta lose right? New city, no kids. If we're gonna have a world war might as well let some guy buy me dinner.

HELEN. How can you do that?

SANDY. Depends if I can get outta here tonight.

HELEN. No I mean sit here, texting, talking to your kids when out there –

SANDY. Can't do anything about out there.

HELEN. You work for him.

SANDY. I'm putting three boys through college.

HELEN. But don't you feel some –

SANDY. What?

HELEN....Responsibility.

Beat.

SANDY *closes her laptop.*

SANDY. You know it's always enjoyable when a woman with a cut-glass accent and no real job talks down to you.

HELEN (*shocked*). I wasn't – I didn't mean to talk down –

SANDY. It's not *my* husband in there deciding whether or not to push the button okay.

HELEN *bristles.*

You know why? Cos I don't have a husband. I'm doing this shit myself. And when my rich-ass liberal friends start bitching and moaning and saying things like how you can do it, you're aiding and abetting, are you proud of yourself – you know what I say? I say yeah. I *am* proud of myself. I'm proud that I got out of my shitty neighbourhood, proud that I hauled my ass through school with straight As, proud that I put myself through college and got a job in The *White House* leaving those Harvard guys in the dust – most of whom by the way would've walked into this job on twice the pay, with half the ability and taking *none* of the racist, sexist horseshit I put up with on a daily basis. I'm proud that I can spot and spin a story in less than a half an hour that could have easily sunk this ship and I'm proud that my whole goddamn life is spent saving the asses of people with a lot more money and power than I'll ever have and who never *ever* say thanks.

HELEN.... Thank you.

SANDY. You're welcome.

SANDY *opens her laptop again. Starts typing.*

HELEN. But that man ran a campaign on pure hate. So as far as I'm concerned even by voting for him –

SANDY. Who says I voted for him?

HELEN *stops.*

No, that'd be the ladies that look like you. Guess some people don't know what's good for 'em.

SOPHIA *has appeared at the door.*

(*Brightly.*) Oh there you are! How do you feel about a photo?

SOPHIA. Photo?

SANDY. A visual of you both to send out with this story – which is going very well by the way. Lots of traction.

HELEN (*firm*). I'm not taking part in any photo until I've spoken to my husband.

SANDY. Why?

HELEN. Because I need to know what's going on.

SANDY. Why do you need to know what's going on?

HELEN. Excuse me?

SANDY. Don't they have that saying where you're from – 'when you join the army, you gotta wear the boots'? Least yours are Prada right? I'll go see about a photographer. (*Glancing out window.*) They *seriously* need to clear that street.

SOPHIA *comes into the room and sits down.*

HELEN *watches her, slightly wary.*

HELEN....that was quick.

SOPHIA. I told you. We don't talk much.

HELEN. Why did he want you down there?

SOPHIA. For the same reason he brought me here.

HELEN *looks at her.*

Men are animals. In every room they will sniff out who is the one with the most strength. My husband knows this. He brings me down there because he wants me to admire him.

HELEN. *Admire* him?

SOPHIA. A man who brings his wife to the meeting room and repeats to her what everyone else already knows, boasting of his diplomatic triumph, his negotiating success. This man has power. This man is top dog. This man is giving other men a warning. He will not back down.

HELEN....so you're some kind of... talisman?

SOPHIA. I am a trophy. For his success.

HELEN*'s appalled.*

HELEN. And this doesn't bother you?

SOPHIA *shrugs.*

...well he's getting a bit ahead of himself, isn't he? He hasn't actually been successful yet.

SOPHIA *looks up.*

SOPHIA....They did not tell you?

HELEN. Tell me what?

Beat.

SOPHIA.... Your husband has given his support.

HELEN. What?

SOPHIA. They will go ahead with the strikes.

HELEN. That's not possible.

SOPHIA. And your country will send troops.

HELEN. Troops!

SOPHIA. If it comes to it. Which it will.

HELEN. That's not possible. He would – never agree to that.

SOPHIA. This is not just US problem. It is in Europe's interest to act –

HELEN. You've misunderstood.

HELEN *rushes to the door.*

SOPHIA. They are already back inside.

HELEN *stops.*

She goes to her phone.

There are no phones –

HELEN. I'm calling Georges. Because this is crazy. For god's sake, they've barely been in there an hour.

SOPHIA. Maybe he'd already made up his mind.

HELEN *looks at her.*

She hangs up.

HELEN. He would have told me.

SOPHIA. You have not seen him for forty-eight hours.

HELEN. Of course I've seen him, I saw him today. At lunch.

SOPHIA. But you were talking to the new Chancellor. He is also very much in support.

Beat.

HELEN *stops, realising.*

I prefer the old Chancellor. She always admired my shoes.

HELEN....Why would he agree to this?

SOPHIA *looks at her.*

SOPHIA. He wants to win next election.

HELEN. And he thinks – *this* will?

SOPHIA. He is taking action. Reshaping global alliances. He is putting himself on the map.

HELEN. But this makes him an accomplice.

SOPHIA....It is useful distraction from his personal life.

Silence.

Then –

HELEN....that COWARD!

HELEN *hurls her phone across the room.*

SOPHIA *watches, surprised.*

How dare he do this to me?

SOPHIA....Is it not possible he is doing what he believes is right?

HELEN. He *knows* this isn't right. Refusing to turn his back on desperate refugees who'd made perilous journeys, that was right. Standing up to – populist member states who wanted to shut their doors, that was right. Not caving in to pressure, or talk of terror or attacks, that was right – and you know how he had the balls to do all that? Because I told him to. And now, he tries to – shut me out.

SOPHIA. Perhaps his advisers –

HELEN. His advisers! Little men with pencils, cutting every speech short. Never mind that those speeches helped get him elected.

SOPHIA. So you do write them?

HELEN *doesn't answer.*

And does he take you to his meetings?

HELEN. He used to. Every one.

SOPHIA. But not lately?

HELEN....Not lately, no.

SOPHIA *watches her.*

SOPHIA....It must be frustrating. To see your wisdom being squandered.

HELEN *laughs, hollow.*

HELEN. You know what the most insulting thing about being an older woman is? Wisdom. 'You've such wisdom,' these young ministers love to say. 'You've such insight. It's because of all your years of experience. You've so much to contribute because you've learned so much from life.' It's got nothing to do with learning from life. I've wisdom because I'm smarter than them. I've ideas because I think. I'm not wise because I'm old, I'm wise because I'm better than them. I could wipe the floor with the whole fucking lot of them. Wisdom! Fuck off.

SOPHIA. Everybody knows what you have done for your husband.

HELEN. No they don't.

She stops.

...No, they don't.

Beat.

You know, I see them. These – rare women who make it in politics. The old Chancellor, the old Prime Minister, that nice – one from New Zealand, I see how they look at me. Shaking my hand, admiring my dress. Pretending they care what I think. They don't care what I think. I'm nothing to these women. I'm wallpaper. Something to pass in the hall.

SOPHIA. But they have won elections.

HELEN. *I* have won elections.

Beat.

...is he really going to do this? Without even – after everything we've worked for? Everything I've done, I left a perfectly good marriage for what – for *this*?

SOPHIA. It could not have been such a good marriage.

HELEN. Oh yes it was. My ex-husband was a very good man.

SOPHIA. Then you would have stayed with him.

HELEN. No, see that's the lie. Good men might be good men, but they're not the most exciting. My first husband was decent and kind, he adored me. And how did I repay him?

SOPHIA. You seduced your student.

HELEN *stops*.

This was in the papers in all our countries.

HELEN. I didn't seduce him. He seduced me.

SOPHIA. He seduced –

HELEN. *Yes*. I was forty-one, I was vulnerable.

Beat.

…I was starting to feel old.

SOPHIA. Forty-one is not old.

HELEN. Try telling that to a forty-one-year-old.

And he wasn't my student. He just came to my class one day. We were here for a summer, my family and I, I was giving a – summer school on international media at a French university. Thought it'd be fun.

And some time in the middle of the first week, this – boy. This beautiful boy suddenly turns up in my classroom. He's young and bright, not even at university yet but he's reading everything, every newspaper in every language and he knows everything about politics and history – he is *so* sharp. I envy that mind. And I envy his youth and his energy. And even though I soon realise, he's not supposed to be in my classroom, he hasn't got any money to pay for the course… I let him stay. Because I like him. I can see that if he was just given – a chance… he could be very great indeed.

And on the last day, I take the students out for a drink. And when the others have all gone and it's just me and him, this boy declares that he's in love with me. Says he knows it in his soul. And though I am married and much *much* older and live in an entirely different country – he will wait, he says. For me.

She looks at SOPHIA.

Course I wasn't so delusional as to think he meant it. I laughed him off, went back home. Got that job – finally – as editor for a wonderful publication, lasted eight, nine months… cos we were writing to each other by then. And the letters had taken an erotic – no a *filthy* turn. And he was eighteen now and at university in Paris and I had many friends in Paris so – one weekend I just went. Just took a plane, spent three days with him.

In bed.

Fucking.

And two months later I did what every good mother should not do. I left my fine, unexciting marriage and my beautiful teenage daughter for a man not much older than she was. I cut off *every* life line, lost *every* single friend and I came here and I started again… For him. And all that energy, all that drive that I could've put into my own career, or my marriage or *myself* in my last two energetic decades of life I've poured into him, because I thought, I've probably left it too late to be great. But he hasn't. He still has time. He can be great instead of me – *he's my legacy*. And look what he's just done.

SOPHIA. You found a great passion.

HELEN. I helped create a monster. God, I want to hurt him. I swear – I swear when he comes out of that room and I see him –

SOPHIA. It will be too late.

HELEN *stops*.

…I am sorry.

HELEN *doesn't respond*.

A long silence.

…Though there is – one other possibility?

HELEN. What's that?

SOPHIA. If you helped to create this monster, you can help to destroy him too.

HELEN *looks up.*

You were right when you asked if I wanted something.

HELEN.... You want me to turn against my husband.

Beat.

Why? You've got what you came here for – your country 'defending' itself.

SOPHIA. That is what my husband came here for.

HELEN. Is it not the same thing?

SOPHIA. No.

HELEN *frowns, trying to comprehend.*

A war will not change anything... People think every war is different. Different countries, different religions. But I have seen war. They are all the same. To me there is no difference between those men in the back of the van and those men down the hall. They all want the same thing. To control.

Beat.

But it is you and I who have the real power.

HELEN.... You and I?

HELEN *stares at her.*

Oh, sweetheart... You and I don't have any – actual power... We're relics, you and I. We're *wives*.

SOPHIA.... We are two women in a room with a bottle of poison.

SOPHIA *reaches down and opens her bag.*

She places the bottle of Chanel on the table.

I think there is some power in that.

HELEN *looks at the bottle.*

HELEN. And what do you suggest we do with that?

SOPHIA....A protest.

HELEN (*dry*). A *protest*. Ah yes. Of course.

SOPHIA. You said you wanted to hurt him.

HELEN. Well yes /

SOPHIA. You said you wanted to stop the strikes.

HELEN. And I do.

SOPHIA. And we can. If we have imagination. It takes imagination to create something. It takes imagination to destroy it too. The people who attack my husband's country two weeks ago, the people who fly the planes into the Towers, they had imagination.

HELEN. They were also psychotic.

SOPHIA. It does not change the fact.

HELEN. I'm not sure I understand what you're proposing...

SOPHIA. I am simply pointing out. We are not just two first ladies in back room waiting for men to decide our fate. We can decide our fate. If we choose.

HELEN. We?

HELEN *glances at the bottle*.

You mean... (*Laughs*.) Okay, you're not serious.

SOPHIA. I came here to find an ally.

HELEN. I thought you came because your husband likes to be admired.

SOPHIA. You say that in ourselves we have no power, I agree. We are not elected, we are symbols.

HELEN. Of what, that's the question?

SOPHIA. Of a world where behind every great man is a silent woman in a designer dress. Of a world where every major war has been started by men and suffered by women. We are symbols of a world where after everything we have fought for, after everything we have done, we are still left waiting on sidelines. Doing nothing. Looking on. Well if I am going to be symbol I would like to be one that matters.

Beat.

I want to hurt them too.

HELEN. ...And you think – this will. You think if they come into this room and find – what?

SOPHIA. Two dead first ladies. Yes, I think that will hurt them.

HELEN *stares at her, stunned.*

HELEN *bursts out laughing.*

HELEN. That's – ridiculous.

SOPHIA. ...Why?

HELEN. Why? Because it is. It's insane. Can you imagine?

SOPHIA. I do not think so.

HELEN *keeps laughing.*

How can they drop their bombs then? How can they explain this to their enemies, or media? It cannot be accident that two wives of two of the most powerful men in the world are found dead together the night before a military strike. The world will see it for what it is. A rebellion, a rejection, a protest – the people outside this window, who threw the blood, will know I am not the one who is their enemy. And most of all, and most importantly and the thing that makes me the most happy, everyone will see that our husbands, they are frauds. You want to know how I can go down there, hold his hand, admire him, while he ignores and discards and humiliates me – this is how. I think about the way I will bring him down.

HELEN *has stopped laughing.*

She stares at SOPHIA.

Silence.

HELEN. ...I need a drink.

She goes to the drinks table, shakily turns a bottle. It's empty.

I definitely need a... where's Georges?

She goes to the door, opens it.

SOPHIA *watches*.

Georges! (*To someone outside.*) Is he... no?

She comes back in.

Where's my...

She retrieves her phone.

Taps his number, trying not to look at SOPHIA.

SOPHIA *stays very still. She never takes her eyes off* HELEN.

(*Into phone.*) Georges – hi, just wondering – oh you are? Okay... Yep, see you in a sec.

She hangs up.

On their way up.

SOPHIA. Why do you do that?

HELEN....what?

SOPHIA. Look for distraction.

HELEN. I was just /

SOPHIA. You are unnerved by what I said.

HELEN. Yes, alright. I'm unnerved by it... Fucking terrified actually. An hour ago, you were shaking at the thought of a couple of hundred women in a room, now – I'm starting to wonder if you're a little unhinged.

SOPHIA. Unhinged?

HELEN. Or depressed. Are you depressed?

SOPHIA. I am First Lady. Of course I am depressed.

HELEN. Well... maybe you should take some pills or something. Because this seems like a very – extreme way of dealing with it.

SOPHIA. And what they are planning down the hall is not extreme?

HELEN. Of course it is.

SOPHIA. And your husband changing position to win next election is not extreme?

HELEN. It's abhorrent.

SOPHIA. So you are happy about one form of extremity but not another.

HELEN. *I am not happy about any of it.*

SOPHIA. Then do something about it.

Beat.

Or are you more comfortable hiding in background, letting the real leaders take the risks?

HELEN. That's not fair.

SOPHIA. With your liberal ideas that cost you nothing.

HELEN. Now look –

SOPHIA. Up for the revolution but not for the sacrifice.

HELEN. I've sacrificed.

SOPHIA. Soldiers give up their lives every day.

HELEN. We're not soldiers.

SOPHIA. But we could be.

HELEN. What? /

SOPHIA. And we would not be doing it for one country. We would be doing it for all of them. And every generation after us. We would be symbols that actually stand for something.

Beat.

Or is your husband the only one who can be great?

Silence.

They stare at one another.

The door opens and SANDY *and* GEORGES *walk in.*

SANDY. Okay, we've got some options for you – little left-field but Georges was too pussy to come up here on his own so –

HELEN. We need alcohol.

SANDY. Alcohol? Sure but first –

HELEN. *Now.*

GEORGES *and* SANDY *glance at one another.*

SANDY.…Any particular kind?

SOPHIA. I would like some Champagne.

SANDY (*surprised*). Champagne!

GEORGES. Are we celebrating?

HELEN. No.

SANDY. Well we might be when you guys hear this –

HELEN. I *really* just need that drink.

GEORGES *makes to go.*

GEORGES. I will see what I can –

HELEN (*firm*). No, *you stay.*

GEORGES *stops.*

He glances at SANDY *, uncertain.*

SANDY. Okay. Okay, I can see there's a need…

She makes a face at GEORGES.

Georges, can I leave you to… (*Mouthing.*) sell this.

GEORGES *nods.*

I'll see what I can find.

She goes.

GEORGES *looks at the two ladies, sensing the tension.*

GEORGES. We uh… we have a little proposal…

HELEN *puts a hand to her forehead, stressed.*

HELEN. Oh god.

GEORGES *clocks it, loses his nerve.*

He spots the Chanel on the table.

GEORGES. Ah, you still have the... I love this one. Reminds me of my grandmother.

He gestures he wants to pick up the bottle.

(*To* SOPHIA.) May I?

HELEN *looks at* SOPHIA, *registering the danger.*

HELEN. Oh well, I don't think –

SOPHIA. Of course.

HELEN *glances at* SOPHIA, *panicked.*

SOPHIA *stares back, calm.*

GEORGES *picks up the bottle, oblivious.*

GEORGES. Like the First Lady, my grandmother was a very elegant woman.

HELEN *watches him, tense.*

She would sit at her dressing table and dab just a little behind each ear.

HELEN (*quietly*). Georges...

He continues, oblivious.

GEORGES. She was very delicate, my grandmother. Never too much. Perfume is better when it is light, yes?

HELEN. Georges.

GEORGES (*oblivious*). And that smell – oh, that smell, I will never forget.

He goes to remove the lid but HELEN *pounces on him.*

HELEN. No no no no no no no /

GEORGES. What are you doing /

HELEN. Put it down. Put it down. Put it down. Put it DOWN /

HELEN *snatches the bottle and slams it on the table.*

She steps away from it.

GEORGES *stares at her, alarmed*.

GEORGES. What is the matter with you?

HELEN *steps back, silent*.

GEORGES *glances at* SOPHIA, *unnerved*.

…Has something – happened?

SOPHIA *doesn't respond*.

(*To* HELEN.) Are you alright?

HELEN (*quietly*). I don't know…

HELEN *moves away from him, trying to keep it together*.

GEORGES *continues, uncertain*.

GEORGES.…We have had a request for an interview.

HELEN*'s head comes up*.

HELEN. Interview?

GEORGES. I am not sure it's such a good idea –

HELEN. What sort of interview?

GEORGES. The BBC. They want to speak with you both.

HELEN *looks at* SOPHIA.

It is not about the talks, don't worry. More the role of a – first lady at such a crucial moment. Sandy thinks it could be –

SOPHIA. No.

HELEN. Yes.

GEORGES. I'm sorry?

HELEN. We'll do it.

SOPHIA. No we will not.

GEORGES *looks from one to the other, confused*.

GEORGES.…I must say this surprises me, Hélène – I expected –

HELEN. I said I'll do it.

SOPHIA. Why?

HELEN. It's an opportunity.

GEORGES. Yes exactly /

SOPHIA. For what?

HELEN. To – *do* something. *Say* something. Have a voice.

GEORGES. Yes, this is what we hoped.

   SOPHIA*'s appalled.*

SOPHIA. You are not serious.

HELEN. You were the one who said we had to act.

SOPHIA. Not like this.

HELEN. Why not like this? We can say what we want.

GEORGES (*nervous*). Well, yes / but –

SOPHIA. And what good will that do?

HELEN. What do you mean?

SOPHIA. What will it that change?

HELEN. Everything, possibly.

SOPHIA. I do not think so.

HELEN. Well I do. This is a genuine chance and if you won't
   take it... I will.

GEORGES. They have requested both of you.

HELEN. Doesn't matter, don't need the both of us. One of us
   will do.

   GEORGES *is suddenly worried.*

GEORGES. Hélène... what are you planning to say?

SOPHIA (*to* HELEN). I think you are making a grave mistake.

HELEN. If this is the only way I can get my husband to listen –

SOPHIA. You will make fool of yourself.

HELEN. No, I might actually save myself. And my husband and this country – who knows? At least I'll be telling the truth which is more than you ever seem willing to do… Because maybe you're just too spineless.

HELEN holds SOPHIA's gaze, a challenge.

SOPHIA takes it in.

Beat.

SOPHIA turns to GEORGES, who has been watching, stunned.

SOPHIA.…Georges?

GEORGES. Hmmn?

SOPHIA. Why don't you tell the President's wife the truth?

GEORGES looks at her, surprised.

GEORGES. Excuse me?

SOPHIA. Why don't you stop lying to the wife of the President? Pretending that you are protecting her, when we both know you are not protecting her. You are protecting someone else.

GEORGES. I don't understand…

SOPHIA turns to HELEN.

SOPHIA. Your husband was not talking with his advisers when the meeting broke this evening.

Suddenly GEORGES seems alarmed.

GEORGES. No, no that is not true –

SOPHIA. I am sorry, you are right.

GEORGES. He was with the minister –

SOPHIA. Yes. He was with one – *particular* minister.

HELEN's face falls.

She looks at GEORGES.

HELEN.…She's here?

GEORGES. It was not like that /

HELEN. She's – *here*?

GEORGES. The President did not want to upset you.

HELEN. Where is she?

GEORGES. She has left, madame. A long time / ago.

HELEN. *Where is she, Georges?*

GEORGES. I swear, madame, I swear that she is gone.

HELEN. ...But she *was* here? The President spoke to her?

GEORGES. Only for a few minutes.

HELEN. Only for a few...

> HELEN *is suddenly very still.*

> *A beat as she takes this in.*

GEORGES. ...I was very uncomfortable deceiving you, madame. If it was not such an important day –

HELEN (*suddenly*). Send the press release.

GEORGES. What?... But the President has not –

HELEN. *Send* it.

> GEORGES *doesn't move.*

I'm instructing you to send it, Georges.

GEORGES. Madame, I cannot.

HELEN. Fine, I'll do it. I've a copy on email.

> *She picks up her phone.*

GEORGES (*panicked*). Madame. You must wait –

HELEN (*scrolling*). Think I've waited long enough, don't you?

GEORGES. But please /

HELEN. So he doesn't want my advice any more, fine /

GEORGES. Just listen /

HELEN. He might be able to push me out of a meeting room, but I do still have some agency.

GEORGES. Hélène /

HELEN. Here it is /

GEORGES. You must not send that. /

HELEN (*about to send*). For god's sake, I'm his wife /

GEORGES (*urgent*). *There is another press release, Hélène.*

HELEN *stops, looks up.*

HELEN....A *different* press release?

GEORGES *slowly nods.*

...What does it say?

GEORGES *shifts, awkwardly, glancing at* SOPHIA.

GEORGES. Madame, this is a private matter between you and the President.

HELEN. She already knows everything.

GEORGES (*nervous*). But I think it is best that you hear it from him.

HELEN. Hear *what* from him?

GEORGES *is deeply uncomfortable.*

GEORGES....The President has great respect for you, madame.

HELEN. Then why hasn't he the balls to tell me he's become a warmonger?

GEORGES. He wants you to have as much dignity in this situation as possible.

She laughs.

HELEN. Dignity? That's what they say when they're burying people.

She stops, realising.

You mean...

GEORGES....The President has to think of his family now, madame.

HELEN. His – *family*?

GEORGES. His future.

HELEN's *blood runs cold.*

You have always wanted what is best for him, he knows that, he is very grateful. He wants to make this as easy as possible.

HELEN. As easy as...

GEORGES. For you.

HELEN *stares at him.*

SANDY *re-enters.*

SANDY. Success! Believe it or not, I actually managed to locate some Champagne in this crematorium.

She takes in the atmosphere.

...What?

HELEN (*quietly*). Get out.

SANDY. Huh?

GEORGES. Hélène, please understand.

HELEN. Get. Out.

SANDY. Is this about the interview? Did you say it's the BBC?

Suddenly HELEN *goes for* GEORGES, *physical, savage, hitting him. Pushing him towards the door.*

HELEN. GET OUT, GET OUT, GET OUT, GET OUT, GET OUT, GET OUT /

SANDY. What the fuck – (*To* GEORGES.) What the hell did you say to her? /

HELEN *pushes them into the hallway.*

GEORGES. I am just doing my job, madame.

HELEN. GET OUT!

SANDY. It's just a little interview.

HELEN. GET OUT!

GEORGES. J'essayais juste de faire mon travail! /

SANDY. Five minutes – tops. /

HELEN *slams the door in their faces.*

The two women are alone again.

Silence.

SOPHIA *looks at* HELEN.

SOPHIA.…You should have let him try the perfume.

HELEN *staggers into the middle of the room, stricken.*

HELEN.…he's getting rid of me.

Beat.

SOPHIA. Yes.

Beat.

HELEN. He doesn't – need me. Any more.

Beat.

SOPHIA. People don't repay their debts. They kill them off.

HELEN *nods, taking this in.*

HELEN.…Do you know what the most – pathetic part is?

Beat.

I would never have left him… Even after today. Even after… everything. I'd have found – some way to stay.

Beat.

See, I really thought I'd got away with it… all the – clichés about men getting better with age, more distinguished, while women just – shrivel and are silenced, I *really* thought I'd got away with it. Had my mind, you see. And my mind was the thing he said he loved. Who needs a body? *My mind.* No one else could give him that… See, I believed him when he said he wanted me. I believed him when he said I would always be enough. I believed him when he said he didn't need a normal life or family, those things were meaningless to people like us, we were different, we were living in a different way – I should have known he'd change his mind someday but… I believed him.

She crumbles.

...He has reduced me.

SOPHIA *silently picks up the Chanel bottle and goes to the drinks table.*

She quietly pours some of the liquid between two glasses.

Then she walks towards HELEN, *holding out a glass.*

HELEN *looks at it.*

Very slowly HELEN *takes it.*

...Will it hurt?

SOPHIA. It will hurt. But only for a moment.

HELEN *looks into the glass.*

HELEN. Is this enough?

SOPHIA. This could kill a whole army.

HELEN....Right.

The two women face one another holding their glasses.

Readying themselves.

SOPHIA. Are you ready?

Beat.

HELEN *nods.*

She brings the glass to her lips, hand shaking. SOPHIA *does the same.*

Then –

HELEN....But how will they know?

SOPHIA *stops.*

How will they know *why*?

SOPHIA. Your husband will know why.

HELEN. But how can we be sure? Shouldn't we leave a – note or something?

SOPHIA. We are leaving them our bodies.

HELEN. It's not enough. They have to know that *they* did this. *They* did this to *us*.

SOPHIA *pulls out a lipstick.*

SOPHIA. I have – this?

HELEN....Lipstick?

SOPHIA. We can write it on the walls.

HELEN. In lipstick?

SOPHIA. Lipstick and perfume. Weapons they will never expect.

SOPHIA *goes to the wall.*

HELEN. What do we say?

SOPHIA. We say – we protest.

SOPHIA *starts to write on the wall in large capital letters.*

HELEN *watches.*

HELEN (*quietly*). We protest?

SOPHIA. We protest.

As SOPHIA *writes –*

We protest the butchery of men.

Beat.

We protest the butchery of power.

HELEN *looks into her glass.*

HELEN. Sophia...

SOPHIA. We protest the butchery of presidents.

HELEN (*a little louder*)....Sophia.

SOPHIA. We protest –

HELEN. Sophia!

SOPHIA *turns.*

...What are we doing?

SOPHIA. More than any leader in that room.

HELEN. But – why? Why should we sacrifice our lives?
    They're not sacrificing theirs.

SOPHIA. They will be disgraced.

HELEN. How do we know?

    Beat.

    How do we know they won't keep their positions? How do
    we know this doesn't just free them up to – take another
    wife? Start another war? Maybe this time with each other.
    Maybe they'll blame each other and your husband will think
    I murdered you and start a war with my country or maybe
    the other way round.

SOPHIA. No /

HELEN. But how do we know? They're men.

    Beat.

    If we want to hurt them. We have to hurt *them*. That's the
    only thing they understand.

SOPHIA. There is no way to do that.

HELEN. There must be some way.

SOPHIA. They are in a meeting room surrounded by security.
    There are guards up and down these halls.

HELEN. But you were there earlier. You could go again.

SOPHIA. And what?

HELEN. I don't know – put it in their water? Or their coffee or
    their tea?

SOPHIA. And they would not see me?

HELEN. Then we'll go to the kitchens.

SOPHIA. We are the most photographed women in the world.

HELEN. Well what about the water supply?

SOPHIA. *This* is the only way. *We* have to be the statement. The
    end of the world as they know it. We are drawing the line
    with our lives.

HELEN....Well I can't.

SOPHIA looks at her.

I won't.

HELEN puts the glass down.

Not for them.

She walks to the chair and sits down.

SOPHIA watches her.

SOPHIA. This is because of your daughter.

HELEN slowly takes off her shoes.

You do not want to leave her behind?

HELEN. You give me far too much credit as a mother, Sophia. I left my poor daughter behind years ago. My daughter doesn't owe me a thing.

Beat.

...I'm just a coward.

She sits back, defeated.

SOPHIA looks at her drink, contemplating.

Then, slowly she puts it down too.

She comes and sits opposite HELEN.

SOPHIA. So they have defeated us.

Beat.

Now we are just two women. Sitting in a room. Talking about men.

HELEN. Talking about power.

SOPHIA. It's a different thing?

HELEN....Sadly not.

Beat.

We're the least important people in this building.

A knock on the door.

Oh, fuck off, Georges!

The door opens and the CATERING ASSISTANT *peers in, tentative.*

CATERING ASSISTANT. Je suis désolée…

HELEN *stands, quickly.*

HELEN. Oh god, I'm so sorry. C'est moi qui suis désolée.

CATERING ASSISTANT. Vous avez commandé du Champagne?

HELEN. Champagne. It's the… Oui, oui. Entrez.

The CATERING ASSISTANT *carefully carries a tray with Champagne and two glasses into the room. She stops at the table. Looks at the Chanel bottle and the two glasses.*

CATERING ASSISTANT.…Ici?

HELEN *quickly moves the things to one side.*

HELEN. Oui, parfait.

They watch, a little dazed, as the CATERING ASSISTANT *puts the tray down and arranges the glasses. When she's finished, she looks at them expectantly.*

(*To* SOPHIA.) Oh I don't have any change, do you…

SOPHIA *reaches for her handbag.*

The CATERING ASSISTANT *waits as* SOPHIA *rustles in her purse.*

Suddenly –

CATERING ASSISTANT.…Excusez-moi?

Both women look up, surprised. The CATERING ASSISTANT *tentatively takes her phone out.*

Je pourrais avoir une photo… avec vous?

She gestures to SOPHIA.

HELEN. Oh. She wants a picture with you.

SOPHIA. Oui, bien sûr vous pouvez avoir une photo.

CATERING ASSISTANT (*delighted*). Merci.

SOPHIA. Où voulez-vous que je me mette?

HELEN (*taken aback*). You speak French?

SOPHIA. I speak four languages.

CATERING ASSISTANT. I speak five.

The two ladies are taken aback.

English... just a little.

HELEN. Would you prefer we spoke in English?

The CATERING ASSISTANT *shrugs, hands* HELEN *her phone.*

Oh, I see. I'm the... right.

The CATERING ASSISTANT *and* SOPHIA *stand beside one another a little awkwardly.*

The CATERING ASSISTANT *beams, as* HELEN *holds up the camera.*

Ready?

The CATERING ASSISTANT *nods.*

A series of undramatic clicks.

Okay I think that's...Do you want to check?

The CATERING ASSISTANT *comes over and looks at the pictures.*

She gives HELEN *the thumbs-up. She smiles.*

CATERING ASSISTANT....For my mother.

HELEN. Ah. Where's your mother?

The CATERING ASSISTANT *looks at her.*

CATERING ASSISTANT....I don't know... But she would like.

HELEN. What's your name?

CATERING ASSISTANT. Fatima.

HELEN. When did you – come to this country, Fatima?

FATIMA *looks suddenly worried*.

FATIMA. I have work permit.

HELEN. Oh yes –

FATIMA. The security in Paris, they make big check –

HELEN. Of course, we weren't –

FATIMA. I will be citizen.

HELEN *takes that in*.

HELEN. …Would you like some Champagne?

FATIMA *is confused*. HELEN *holds up the bottle*.

FATIMA (*unsure*). Non non, merci –

HELEN. Just a little drop. Unless you don't –

FATIMA *backs away, alarmed*.

FATIMA. I work now.

HELEN. It's alright, we won't tell anyone.

FATIMA. I work now. I bring the coffee to the Presidents.

HELEN *stops*.

HELEN. …What?

FATIMA. The meeting it will break. I bring the coffee to the Presidents.

SOPHIA *and* HELEN *look at one another*.

FATIMA *stands awkwardly for a moment, then decides to go*.

Okay.

HELEN. Wait!

FATIMA *turns*.

Beat.

(*Slowly*.) Can you… help us?

FATIMA (*uncertain*). Me?… Help – you?

> HELEN *puts the champagne down.*

> *Very slowly she picks up the bottle of Chanel No. 5, holding it in both hands.*

> *She stares at it for a moment, weighing it up.*

> *Then she holds the bottle out towards* FATIMA.

> SOPHIA *watches, surprised.*

HELEN (*slowly*). Can you take this… and put a little – in every coffee pot, every tea pot, every jug of water in that room – with the Presidents?

> FATIMA *stares at her, uncertain.*

> *It's unclear if she understands.*

> Vous pouvez prendre ce flacon et verser un peu dans toutes les cafetières, toutes les théières –

FATIMA. Yes, yes I understand.

SOPHIA. And when you have finished, you will bring this bottle back. To us.

HELEN. Ramenez nous le flacon. A *nous*.

> SOPHIA *takes out some money, hands it to* FATIMA.

SOPHIA. You understand?

> FATIMA *looks at* HELEN, *anxious.*

FATIMA.…It is – a game? …With your husband?

> HELEN *thinks for a moment.*

HELEN.… Yes.

> *Beat.*

> Yes, that's right…

> *Beat.*

> It's all a game to our husbands really.

> *Beat.*

They just don't realise we're players yet.

HELEN *looks at the bottle of Chanel, then gently but firmly she places it in* FATIMA*'s hands.*

Whatever you do. Don't touch it.

FATIMA (*uncertain*)....is perfume?

HELEN *opens her mouth.*

SOPHIA. Just bring this bottle back.

HELEN. And if anyone stops you and asks what it's in it – you say you don't know.

SOPHIA. Et si quelqu'un t'arrête, et demande ce qu'il y a dedans, dis que tu ne sais pas.

HELEN. You can say the ladies sent you.

HELEN *looks at* FATIMA*, urgent.*

Do you understand?

FATIMA *nods.*

FATIMA....Les deux femmes, oui.

Beat.

FATIMA *turns to go.*

As she does, she catches sight of the snow outside the window.

She stops, points.

Ah... Snowing.... We don't see in my country – at this time.

HELEN. We don't see it in this country this time of year either. Certainly not on the Côte d'Azur.

FATIMA *looks at her.*

FATIMA. World is – upside down, yes?

HELEN. Yes.

FATIMA *turns and heads for the door.*

She notices the writing on the wall and stops briefly.

She glances back at them, uncertain.

Come straight back.

FATIMA *nods, and hurries out. The two women are alone again.*

HELEN *walks to the window, looks out.*

SOPHIA *sits down on a chair.*

Silence.

SOPHIA. It is dark outside?

HELEN. Getting there.

SOPHIA. And the protesters?

HELEN....Gone.

Beat.

Will she do it?

SOPHIA. I don't know.

HELEN. What if she tells someone?

SOPHIA. I don't know.

HELEN. Is it really poison?

SOPHIA....I don't know.

HELEN *turns.*

HELEN. Are you afraid?

SOPHIA....No.

HELEN. There are women in that meeting room too.

SOPHIA. Only a few.

SOPHIA *takes out the lipstick.*

She is about to put it on, but instead holds it out towards HELEN.

HELEN *takes it. A beat.*

Suddenly she smears the lipstick across her face.

She turns, and barefoot goes to the wall, looking up at
SOPHIA's *inscription.*

She finishes whatever part of the inscription SOPHIA *has*
left hanging.

The clock ticking becomes a little louder.

HELEN *comes back and takes the seat opposite* SOPHIA.

She hands SOPHIA *back the lipstick.* SOPHIA *takes in*
HELEN's *smeared face.*

Then she carefully runs the lipstick over her own lips, flicks
her hair, straightens her dress, crosses her legs and places
her bag on her lap – impeccable.

HELEN *picks up her glass of champagne, looks at* SOPHIA.

HELEN. Now what?

SOPHIA *looks back at her.*

SOPHIA....We wait.

Beat.

HELEN. We wait.

Black.

www.nickhernbooks.co.uk

facebook.com/nickhernbooks

twitter.com/nickhernbooks